Peasant's Alphabet

More of the best from
The Urban Peasant

James Barber

Recipes from the popular television cooking series

W9-CCZ-431

For Christina…malgré tout.

ACKNOWLEDGEMENTS

Editor: Linda Conway

Design and Production: Judson Young

Production Assistant: Kim Hanen

Project Coordination: Shelley McGaw

Recipe Development and Research: Anik See

Cover Photography: John D. Kenny

Illustrations: Grahame Arnould

1st printing

Distributed by Raincoast Books

Copyright © Urban Peasant Productions Ltd. 1997

All rights reserved

ISBN 0-9698398-4-7

Table of Contents

APPLES, AVOCADOS AND AIOLI

n the south of France, in the evenings of the long soft days of summer, even the clocks are lazy and it sometimes seems that the only signs of movement are the vegetables growing. The villages and small towns are quiet, still sleepy from the afternoon nap, and in some of them— indeed, at some times, most of them—they are waiting for the *aioli monstre* to take over their streets. And, for a short and unforgettable while, their lives.

An *aioli monstre* is not a Jurassic dinosaur. Originally the traditional French feast to celebrate the success of the revolution and the fall of the Bastille, it has now become a summer celebration in its own right, a sort of midsummer harvest festival, usually held on saints' days, which the French have a lot of. Generally, it's a loosely planned street party which everybody, old and young, joins in. Neighbouring villages are careful not to have their celebrations on the same day as their neighbours, so if you're travelling in the region during summer, you have a fair chance of finding yourself in the middle of one of these affairs, eating and drinking yourself into a small but contented coma of unforgettable gluttony.

Aioli is garlic mayonnaise. Nothing from a jar, but *honest* mayonnaise made with eggs and oil, lots of garlic and a strong right arm for beating. It's the most popular quick sauce in southern France because it goes with almost everything. I've eaten it with vegetables, chicken and fish, potatoes fried and potatoes boiled, salads, olives, squid and even spread thick on bread. But best of all, *aioli* goes with salt cod, the thick white fillets of fish that once fed the seamen of the navies of the world, and has now joined the long list of humble, simple foods that appear on the menus of expensive restaurants.

However, if you're not in France, and have some seven or eight friends, access to any of the local markets, a few bottles of wine and the urge to have a good messy, thoroughly satisfying party, then you can have your own *aioli monstre*. Eat, drink and be merry, dance, sing, lie and *finally* kiss your friends on both cheeks, full but not bankrupt, because despite its festive appearance this is not an expensive dish.

Let's start with the *aioli*, the sauce which gives flavour and character to everything else. You need two eggs, four cloves of peeled garlic, a teaspoon (five ml) of any kind of mustard, a good pinch of salt and a half-cup (125 ml) of mild oil, such as safflower or sunflower. Most olive oils are too strong for mayonnaise and will overpower it. I use a food processor or a blender. If you have the muscle, the patience and somebody to help drizzle the oil while you hand beat, odds are you won't need this recipe at all.

Break the eggs into the blender or food processor. Add the garlic, mustard and salt, and run the machine until it looks creamy and smooth. With the machine still running, slowly drizzle in a thin stream of oil, stopping pouring for a second or two (but still whizzing) if the sauce looks oily round the edge. The final product is thick, almost solid, lovely smooth and shining, and you'll easily see why it is often called the butter of Provençe.

A good *aioli* will keep in the refrigerator for a week, but it won't freeze, and like any egg-based mayonnaise, it is not recommended for picnics or sandwiches or any other warm, moist place, because it will pick up bacteria even faster than French designers change the length of a skirt hem. The best thing to do with *aioli* is to eat it, in large quantities, immediately.

Everything else to go with it is simple to prepare, and goes on a large platter. Little baby new potatoes, sprinkled copiously with chopped parsley; small spring beets, *not* peeled and with stalks as long as matchsticks left on, boiled for 30 minutes, when the skins will rub off easily; chickpeas, canned or even better—soaked overnight—then cooked with an onion; fresh peas, or broad beans, shelled and plunged in boiling salted water for no more than two minutes; fresh crisp green beans, in the same water for four minutes, then plunged into a bowl of cold water; asparagus, steamed; chicken, barbecued or poached; spicy Italian sausages; thick slices of good bread, toasted on the barbecue; corn, cooked as you do it best; any kind of firm, white fish, poached, fried or barbecued; snails, mussels or clams; hard-boiled eggs; leeks brushed with oil and barbecued; poached salmon (even canned salmon). There is no end to the things that "go" with a good *aioli*, so long as they are fresh, and small, and local, all of which contribute to the simple goodness of the dish.

But, to be authentic, salt cod is *essential*, and if you've previously shied away from those dry, tough looking slabs in the Italian stores, this may be the best time to discover just how delicate a flavour it has when carefully prepared.

A one pound (500 g) slab is enough for four people. Soak it, for 48 hours in a large pot of cold water, changing the water night and morning. Drain the pot, and cover the fish with fresh cold water. Bring it to a boil, and immediately turn the heat to the lowest, so that the pot is just, and barely, simmering. Very fresh salt cod will cook in 10 minutes, thicker, older chunks may take 20, but keep an eye on it and take it out of the water when it starts to flake easily. That's all—it's ready to eat, with the *aioli*. Or it can be barbecued. Just pat it dry after soaking, lightly brush with oil, and barbecue over high heat, turning once, until it flakes. And if salt cod is too daunting, try a three pound (about 1.5 kg) box of frozen squid, thawed, drained, lightly brushed with oil, and barbecued for *no longer* than three minutes, when they'll be tender and delicate, with a texture and flavour reminiscent of lobster. Squid tastes like rubber simply because they have been overcooked.

That's an *aioli monstre*. There are those who say that the combination of eggs, garlic and oil intensifies the alcoholic nature of wine, and those who claim, as the Russians do, that a stomach well lined with oil is the secret of their capacity for vodka. Whichever you believe, red, white or rosé—they all go well with this particular dish.

Vive la France et bonnes vacances…

Apples a la Bretonne

1 tsp/5 ml butter
1 apple, cored and
   cut into finger-thick slices
1 Tbsp/15 ml brown sugar

juice of half-a-lemon
1 tsp/5 ml cinnamon
2 Tbsp/30 ml whiskey

Melt the butter in a frypan over medium heat. Lay in the apple rings and sprinkle with brown sugar and lemon juice. Cook until lightly browned and until the sugar has caramelized—about 10 minutes. Sprinkle with cinnamon and whiskey and serve. Serves 2.

Apples and Pork

A country dish from Normandy. Where apples and pork come from...

2 Tbsp/30 ml oil
2 pork chops
1 onion, chopped
2 cloves garlic, chopped

1 apple, peeled and sliced
1/4 cup/60 ml apple juice
1 tsp/5 ml thyme
2 Tbsp/30 ml cream

Heat the oil in a frypan over high heat. Add the pork chops and cook for 2 to 3 minutes until each side is nicely browned. Add the onions and garlic, stir, and then add the apple. Cook for 2 minutes, and stir in the apple juice and thyme. Reduce the heat to medium, cover and let cook 10 minutes. Add the cream, bring to a boil, remove from heat and serve. Serves 2.

Real Guacamole

You know what guacamole is—and it's usually more complicated than this. You know better.

2 avocados, peeled and mashed
1 onion, finely chopped

juice of 1 lime
salt and pepper

Mash the avocado, onion and lime juice together in a bowl with a fork. Season and serve. Makes 2 cups/500 ml.

Spanish Trout with Almond Sauce

One pot, two fish, two people, ten minutes.

24 almonds
1/4 cup/60 ml olive oil
2 cloves garlic
1 tomato, chopped
1 slice stale bread, cubed
1 tsp/5 ml vinegar

1/4 cup/60 ml sherry
   or apple juice
a pinch of cayenne
2 Tbsp/30 ml butter
2 trout
salt and pepper

Toast the almonds over medium to high heat in a dry frypan and set aside. In the same pan, heat half of the oil over high heat and add the garlic, tomato, bread, vinegar and sherry. Cook for 2 to 3 minutes, until the tomatoes and bread have softened. Place the almonds, cayenne and tomato mixture into a food processor and whiz until smooth. Set aside. Heat the butter and the remaining oil in a frypan over high heat. Lay the trout in the frypan and cook for 3 to 4 minutes on each side. Pour the almond sauce over top, season and serve. Serves 2.

Tomato, Apple and Apricot Chutney

This keeps in the fridge for a month or so, and is terrific with curries, or just with some cheese and bread.

1 Tbsp/15 ml oil
2 cloves garlic, chopped
1 tsp/5 ml cinnamon
a pinch of cayenne
1/2 tsp/2.5 ml cloves
1/3 cup/85 ml sugar

1/4 cup/60 ml vinegar
1/4 cup/60 ml water
3 tomatoes, chopped
2 apples, peeled and chopped
1/2 cup/125 ml dried apricots, chopped
salt and pepper

Heat the oil in a saucepan over high heat. Add the garlic, spices, sugar and vinegar and cook for 2 minutes. Add the remaining ingredients, reduce the heat to medium and let them simmer until the apricots are soft-about 20 minutes. If the mixture becomes too dry, add more water and reduce the heat further. Makes about 3 cups/750 ml.

BANANAS, BEER, BABIES AND BEANS

Everybody knows about beans. And everybody knows something different. If you're French Canadian you know about beans on New Year's Eve, a great pot of beans cooked slow in a big pot with salt pork and maple syrup and eaten with *tortiere*, the *Quebecois* pie made with ground pork or sometimes, if it's in the North, with venison.

That's beans, French Canadian style. English Canada's a little different. Sometimes I think we make beans a symbol of poverty— we say things aren't "worth a hill of beans" or "all you'll get there is a can of beans" and everybody understands exactly what we mean.

And then there's the universally accepted concept of beans—accepted the world over because it's true—the old children's rhyme of "Beans, beans the musical fruit, the more you eat, the more you toot".

Nobody thinks it's very polite, but everybody has a quiet laugh about it; fart is one of those words that isn't taught in "English as a Second Language" classes, and until very recently it was the *one* four-letter-word that the CBC wouldn't use.

But, suddenly the word is socially acceptable. People are talking about it and using it in normal conversation. "FART", they say and nobody giggles, because now it's become serious.

It seems that a professor, one Professor Brimacombe, at the University of East Anglia, has finished a study of er…farts…and he has discovered that not only do they corrode and tarnish silverware, but they also darken the pigment of paintings. He wants art galleries to take notice of this effect, and to do something about it.

Apparently, farting has a lot to do with what you eat, and beans aren't the only culprit involved. Vegetarians do it more than meat-eaters, and winter foods produce more than summer foods. Since more people go to art galleries in winter than in summer, and since they've all been eating winter food (potatoes and spinach are highly fart productive, and so are eggs and cheese and onions) there they are, all walking around, looking at the paintings…*and doing it*! Quietly or loudly, the good professor doesn't say. But he has measured—and we certainly don't know how—the chemical composition of a fart and he reports that the average one contains two to three milligrams of hydrogen sulphide, and *that's* what turns the silver black, *that's* what messes up the paintings!

Professor Brimacombe also says that wet raincoats accentuate the problem. Makes it last longer, if you understand. Wet raincoats can be dealt with—they must be checked at the door, but the other problem…? He suggests that people, as he puts it, exercise "a modicum of restraint". This may be polite, but I'm not sure it's entirely safe. I do remember a gravestone in a Yorkshire churchyard, on which was carved:

> "Where e'er you be
> let your wind go free.
> Here lies the body of Joshua Pinn
> Who died a sad death from holding it in."

Fried Bananas

2 Tbsp/30 ml butter
2 bananas,
  peeled and halved lengthwise

1 Tbsp/15 ml sugar
2 Tbsp/30 ml rum or whiskey
whipped cream or ice cream

Melt the butter in a frypan over medium heat. Add the bananas and sugar and cook for 2 to 3 minutes or until the bananas have softened slightly. Turn the bananas over and cook for 2 more minutes. Splash lightly with rum, and serve with whipped cream or a scoop of ice cream on the side. Serves 2.

Bread and Butter Pudding

8 thick slices white bread,
  preferably stale
3 Tbsp/45 ml butter, softened
3 eggs

2 Tbsp/30 ml sugar
2 cups/500 ml milk
4 squares semi-sweet chocolate,
  cut into chunks

Preheat your oven to 375F (190C). Butter the pieces of bread and place butter-side down in a baking dish. Beat the eggs, sugar and milk together and pour over the bread. Scatter chocolate chunks over the top. Dot with any remaining butter and bake for 30 minutes, until browned and set. Serves 4.

White Bean Ful

In Egypt, these beans are a popular breakfast dish, but are also sometimes puréed and served as a dip.

1-14 oz/398 ml tin white beans,
  drained and rinsed
2 tomatoes, chopped
1 cup/250 ml parsley, chopped
1/3 cup/85 ml oil

5 cloves garlic, chopped
zest and juice of 2 lemons
4 hard-boiled eggs
salt and pepper

Purée all of the ingredients together and serve with pita bread, hard-boiled eggs and lemon wedges. Serves 4 as an appetizer.

Black Bean and Banana Soup

Soul food in 15 minutes.

2 Tbsp/30 ml oil
1 onion, chopped
2 cloves garlic, chopped
2 Tbsp/30 ml oregano
2 tsp/10 ml cumin
2 tomatoes, chopped
2 chilis, chopped

2 bananas, peeled and chopped
2-14 oz/398 ml tins black beans,
   drained and rinsed
1/2 cup/125 ml stock or water
a handful of cilantro, chopped
salt and pepper

Heat the oil in a large pot over high heat. Add the onion, garlic and spices. Cook for 2 to 3 minutes, then add the tomatoes, chilis and one of the bananas. Cook for 2 minutes, stir in the black beans, stock and cilantro. Bring to a boil, reduce the heat to medium and cook for 10 more minutes. For a smooth soup, purée the soup in a food processor or blender; for a chunkier soup, leave just as is. Season and serve with cilantro and remaining chopped banana sprinkled over top. Serves 4.

Beer and Cheese Fondue

Hockey night, the big game, or just a party.

2 Tbsp/30 ml butter
2 cloves garlic, finely chopped
2 Tbsp/30 ml flour
1 bottle beer

2 1/2 cups/625 ml
   cheddar cheese, grated
1 tsp/5 ml dried chilis
1 tsp/5 ml dry mustard
a pinch of nutmeg

Melt the butter in a saucepan and stir in the garlic. Add the flour and stir until smooth. Pour in the beer, stirring all the time and bring to a boil. Add the grated cheese and spices. When everything is all melted, turn the heat down very low and keep warm. Cut up some raw vegetables or good bread and serve with the fondue. Serves 4 as an appetizer.

Chicken in Beer

6 chicken thighs
2 Tbsp/30 ml cornstarch
4 slices bacon, chopped
1 onion, chopped
2 cloves garlic, chopped

1 bottle beer
1 tsp/5 ml thyme
1 bay leaf
2 Tbsp/30 ml butter
salt and pepper

Shake the chicken thighs in a bag with the cornstarch until well-coated. Place the bacon in a frypan over high heat. Fry for 2 to 3 minutes, turn over and add the chicken thighs, onion and garlic. Cook the chicken for 3 minutes on each side until lightly browned. Add the beer, thyme and bay leaf. Cover and simmer for 20 minutes. Remove the chicken and onions, and add the butter. Boil the sauce for 1 minute after the butter has melted. Season and serve the chicken and sauce over rice. Serves 2.

Pasta Fagioli

A classic dish from Tuscany...dead easy and very comforting.

2 Tbsp/30 ml oil
6 cloves garlic, left whole
2 carrots, chopped
1 red onion, chopped
3 stalks celery, chopped
1 tsp/5 ml salt
pepper
a handful of basil, chopped

1-28 oz/796 ml tin white beans,
   drained and rinsed
1 cup/250 ml small pasta
   (like macaroni)
4 cups/1 litre water or stock
zest and juice of 1 lemon
parmesan cheese
1/2 a bunch of parsley, chopped

Heat the oil in a large saucepan over medium-high heat and add the garlic and vegetables. Toss, add seasonings and cook for 3 minutes. Add the beans, pasta and water, then bring to a boil and reduce the heat to low. Simmer for 20 minutes. Add the lemon, stir and serve sprinkled with parmesan and parsley. Serves 4.

CABBAGE
IS
CHEAP

Cabbage costs somewhere around 35 cents a pound and there's never any shortage of it. Supermarkets, corner stores and local markets; they've all got cabbage, and just about every society in the world has special recipes for it, but in North America we seem to think only of cabbage rolls or coleslaw. The Indonesians make *gado-gado*, a cabbage based salad with peanuts; the Koreans ferment it, spike it up with vinegar and hot red peppers and call it *Kim Chee*. The Hungarians make a great warming borscht of cabbage, while the French make sauerkraut for special occasions, surrounded with smoked meat and sausages and, if you're lucky, liberally doused with champagne. All good Chinese restaurants serve half-a-dozen varieties of cabbage (*Bok Choy*, *Sui Choy*, *Choy Sam*, *Gai Lan* or whatever else is in season), and they eat it as a delicacy, with the same reverence as we accord asparagus.

The Romanians stuff cabbage leaves with ground meat and rice, which is something they learned from the Greeks, who use grape leaves and call them *dolmades*. Cantonese cooks do much the same with lotus leaves. The British, as every stand-up comedian knows, boil cabbage into a yellow stinking mess, and the occasional food writer will discover—about the time of Valentine's Day—that cabbage contains theobromine, and theobromine is the ingredient in chocolate which seems to have been proven to accelerate the libido.

However, "*Cabbage Makes You Horny*" is a headline *not* destined to appear even in *The National Enquirer*, and certainly not in the pages of the glossy food magazines. Even comfort cooking (all the recipes that got your forbears through the depression of the Thirties)

manages to avoid cabbage, except for the occasional dish of corned beef in a pub.

But if it's January, the last of the turkey is gone, the temperatures are low, and so is the cash flow, cabbage is *still* 35 cents a pound. So herewith a small collection of one-pot, simple, ridiculously inexpensive cabbage recipes, really comforting winter suppers which not only taste good but also *feel* good.

First of all, the simplest of all—a garlic sausage, a cabbage and a big saucepan with a lid. You can make it for two or for six, but since it reheats very well, in a microwave, a conventional oven or even the same pot it was cooked in (just add a little bit of water to make steam), you might just as well make a big pot; it takes no longer than a small one.

Slice the garlic sausage as thick as your finger. Quarter the cabbage and cut out the wedge of solid core at the bottom. Slice the cabbage crosswise (also as thick as your finger) and heat two tablespoons (30 ml) of vegetable oil in the pan over medium to high heat. Add the sausage slices, stir and toss them a minute, then add the sliced cabbage and toss well to coat everything with hot oil (get the spatula underneath). Add a little beer, or water, or stock (I would say four tablespoons (60 ml), but I've never associated beer with tablespoons), and sprinkle copiously with coarse ground black pepper. Lid on, heat down to low, cook 20 minutes and there's supper. If you want to be sophisticated, add a good sprinkling of caraway seeds with the beer. If you want to be Pennsylvania Dutch, add a big green apple, cored and coarse-chopped with the caraway seeds, and stir in a tablespoon (15 ml) of vinegar for the last five minutes of cooking. If you want to be French then use butter instead of oil, and if you want to stretch your dollar even further, then serve the beer you're going to drink with it in wine glasses—it goes a lot further.

Now, equally cheap, equally simple, and equally quick to make, a winter meal from Southwestern France, where at this time of year the women of the district sharpen their knives, and the pigs stop grunting, to become hams, bacon, sausages and any one of the hundreds of other delicacies (from soup to nuts) that can be made from the spare parts of a pig.

I don't know what it's called, but just outside Toulouse, in the village of Escancrabe (population 273) it is generally known as "lunch", and right after breakfast it goes on the stove, or close to the fire, or in a slowly cooling mud-brick oven that was used earlier to bake bread. For two or four hours it sits there, making a rich, warm, soft and loving smell, and at noon the men come in from the fields to eat it. Lunch is the focal point of the day down there—*everything* stops; the tractors in the fields, the trucks on the road and the kids in the schools. From 11:30 am on, the standard greeting from anybody you meet is "On your way to lunch?" One year, when a man was killed by a cow rolling on him at 11:45 am, there was great sympathy expressed in the community: "*Poor guy—hadn't even had his lunch…*"

This doesn't have to be lunch. It makes a great supper on weekends, takes 10 minutes to prepare and will cook quite happily in two hours, while you watch the ball game, take a bath or walk the cat. It doesn't need a wood-burning fireplace or a country oven— even with a simple electric stove it will still make the most celibate of bachelor suites smell like a rural farmhouse, especially if you can see the North Shore mountains and pretend they're the Pyrenees.

You can cook it on top of the stove or in the oven, and all it needs to make it complete is a loaf of good bread and a bottle of good dark cheap red (you really can't go wrong with something from Chile or Portugal). You can find enormously complicated recipes for *chou farci* (stuffed cabbage) but this very simple one-pot special is a lot easier.

Here's what you do, for six people: One cabbage, four to five pounds (about two kg), two pounds (one kg) pork sausage meat or pork sausages, pepper and salt and about three ounces (100 g) of butter. Those are the ingredients, no more, no less; no herbs, no fancies.

Halve the cabbage, cut out the core, slice it crosswise into slices two-fingers thick, and drop them into a pan full of boiling, salted water. Let it boil fast for four or five minutes, then run it under the cold tap to stop cooking, and drain it. Butter the inside of a pot wider than deep, lay in a third of the cabbage, then half the sausage meat (if they're sausages take the skins off). Pepper it copiously, and salt, but remember you can always add it later. Cover with another third of the cabbage, more pepper and salt, then the rest of the sausage meat. Finish with the remainder of the cabbage, and cut the butter into little bits to dot over the top. Put the lid on tight (if you don't have a lid then seal it with foil, but make sure it's tight so the juices stay in). Put it on top of the stove for two or three hours, barely simmering on very low heat, or bake it in a 300F (150C) oven for the same time.

Left-overs reheat well (I sometimes eat slabs of it cold for breakfast) so don't bother making a small version of it. Go all the way, invite a few friends, and, male or female, enjoy being Earth Mother.

And, remember, although cabbage is only 35 cents a pound, you don't need to be ashamed of it. If you need some sort of intellectual or emotional support to serve it, halfway through dinner you could quietly steer the conversation to classical music, and find your opportunity to discuss Johann Sebastian Bach *and* cabbage. It seems that *The Goldberg Variations* are based on an old German folk song with the recurrent refrain of: "Cabbage, cabbage, makes you fart".

Cabbage and Canned Salmon, Korean-style

This got invented sailing up from San Francisco in bad weather. Very quick, very good.

2 Tbsp/30 ml oil
1/2 inch/1.25 cm fresh ginger, chopped
1 onion, chopped
1 small cabbage, cored and chopped

1-7 oz/196 g tin salmon, drained
salt and pepper
1 Tbsp/15 ml sesame oil

Heat the oil in a frypan over high heat and stir in the ginger. Add the onion and cabbage and cook for about 10 minutes. Add the salmon, salt and pepper and stir. Cook for 2 to 3 minutes, drizzle with sesame oil and serve. Serves 2.

Minestrone with Basil

3 Tbsp/45 ml oil
1 onion, chopped
2 cloves garlic, chopped
2 cups/500 ml green cabbage, chopped
1 carrot, chopped
1 celery stalk, chopped
2 tomatoes, chopped

1 potato, peeled and chopped
5 cups/1.25 litres water
1-14 oz/398 ml tin kidney beans, drained and rinsed
1/2 cup/125 ml macaroni
1/2 cup/125 ml basil, chopped
1 tsp/5 ml salt
parmesan cheese

Heat the oil in a large pot over medium heat. Add the onion and garlic and cook for 2 to 3 minutes or until softened. Add the cabbage, carrot, celery, tomatoes and potato and cook for 2 minutes. Stir in the water and beans and bring to a boil. Cook, covered, for about 10 minutes. Add the pasta and cook for 10 more minutes. Stir in the basil, season with salt and serve with cheese sprinkled over top. Serves 4.

County Cork Cabbage Soup

St. Patrick's Day, or once a month in winter.

2 Tbsp/30 ml butter
1 small cabbage, cored
   and sliced very thin
1 onion, chopped
2 cups/500 ml stock
1 potato, peeled and grated

2 Tbsp/30 ml flour
3 cups/750 ml milk
a pinch of ground cloves
salt and pepper
1/4 cup/60 ml parsley,
   chopped

Melt the butter in a large pot over medium heat. Add the cabbage and onion and cook for 5 minutes. Add the stock, potato and flour. Stir and cook for 2 minutes. Add the milk and ground cloves and bring to a boil. Cook 20 minutes while stirring occasionally. Season and serve sprinkled with parsley. Serves 4.

Bubble and Squeak

Classic British leftovers, squeaks and bubbles as it cooks.
Any leftover greens will do instead of the cabbage.

1/4 cup/60 ml butter
2 cups/500 ml leftover cooked
   cabbage, chopped
1 egg, beaten

2 cups/500 ml leftover
   potatoes, mashed
1 Tbsp/15 ml pepper

Melt the butter in a frypan over medium heat. In a large bowl, combine the remaining ingredients, and mix them together until well-combined. Place the mixture in the frypan and pat down into a cake. Reduce the heat to low and cook until the bottom has browned—about 15 minutes. Invert a plate over the top of the frypan and flip the cake out onto the plate. Eat just as is, or slip the cake back into the frypan and cook the other side for 2 to 3 minutes and serve. Serves 2.

DIETS
AND
DESSERTS

It's all too easy to get fat. And the world is full of remedies. Some will have you eat grapefruit, some will have you eat only steak, some will sell you pills and others will give you a list of *good* food and *bad* food, together with a calorie counter, and a daily chart of exactly when and what you should eat.

In case you didn't know, getting thin was a $30 billion industry last year in the United States. It's a guilt industry, and without going into the complicated reasons of why people want to be thin, it's interesting to realize that while 70 percent of women with normal weight say they want to be thinner, 23 percent of underweight women have the same ambition. Even *imagined* fat is somehow wrong, and while women are the main subscribers to this doctrine, men are not insignificant members of the congregation of guilt. According to American statistics, 50 percent of women and 30 percent of men are always on some kind of diet.

But, we're not all that different in Canada. We worry, as much as anybody else in the world (last year, in Thailand, a country of mostly small and delicate people, there were stickers in Bangkok advertising weight loss workshops). We know the joys and pleasures of cream, the satisfaction of rich things, and we eat them, almost as though there will never be another chance. It takes a lot of willpower to successfully resist dessert, and it's a great triumph for most of us to take our imaginations past whipped cream, and booze, and chocolate. All you have to do is just say "*Black Forest Cake*" or "*Cheesecake*", let alone that wonderfully titled, very popular restaurant dessert "*Death By Chocolate*", and mouths begin to water.

But dessert is the best place to start *not* putting on pounds. Saying "No" is hard, particularly after a good dinner, when everyone is in a self-indulgent mood. And weddings, birthday parties, family get-togethers are not the time to introduce family and friends to your guilt. But in your own home there are lots of ways to start paring off a few pounds, and what's more, feeling good about it.

People's food habits are largely inherited from their grandparents. Canadian food established itself early on when the settlers were busy clearing land, building boats, chopping down trees and being generally busy outdoors. Meat and potatoes, fried food, big chunks of cake, stacks of hotcakes. We went in for what an 1890's cookbook I was recently looking at called "*Good Dinners For Men*".

Those dinners still exist, in fishing camps, in logging camps and on construction sites, where people are seriously burning calories 10 or 12 hours a day, and need regular refuelling. When I worked in construction camps, the kitchen always ordered four pounds of steak per man, per meal, and there were no leftovers—everything got eaten.

In one camp we had a cook who tried to introduce change; to make soups and serve two percent milk instead of the cans of condensed milk that were our regular fare. He steamed fish instead of frying it, and he made the awful mistake one day of serving tofu. They ran him out of camp after a week.

The food magazines are full of references to the "Mediterranean Diet", which really means eating the way that a lot of people have done for years. The Italians, the Greeks, the Spaniards—all the people who live in sunny warm climates where olives grow, and sheep are milked, where the hillsides grow grapes and the valleys produce lots of fruit.

And it's not just on the Mediterranean that people are living on this kind of simple food. The Middle East, a lot of India, Southern Russia and Turkey all share much the same ingredients in their diet. A lot less meat, more oil, fresh fruit and vegetables—that's a common shopping list. But the one ingredient common to them all is yoghurt.

So let's start there, with yoghurt. Not as a *substitute* for but as an *alternative* to whipped cream. Whipping cream has 35 to 40 percent of butterfat, yoghurt from one to 10 percent, and is particularly well suited for summer desserts—it has a slight acidity which emphasizes the sweetness of fruit or even a rhubarb crumble. (And it never hurts to remember that you usually get what you pay for. *Good* yoghurt costs more than not-so-good.)

Instead of mayonnaise, made of egg yolks and lots of oil, dressings made of yoghurt are light and fresh and ridiculously easy to make. A cup (250 ml) of yoghurt, a handful of chives chopped fine, a good sprinkle of pepper and maybe one half-teaspoon (2.5 ml) of mustard. There's a wonderful instant dressing for any kind of salad, for a piece of fish or even barbecued chicken.

Mix yoghurt with chopped parsley, with a little curry powder, a sprinkle of pepper and another of oregano, thin it out a little with a spoonful or so of water and spoon it over fresh sliced juicy tomatoes. Stir beet juice (from a jar of pickled beets is fine) into yoghurt and you have a pink dressing which will delight the kids and get them to eat their spinach.

Sprinkle a little brown sugar over a small bowl of yoghurt, and let it sit, undisturbed for a couple of hours or overnight in the fridge. The sugar will slowly melt down into the yoghurt, and you'll end up with a pretty, marbled dessert which needs nothing more than a few wedges of fresh-sliced apple arranged on it, and a dusting of cinnamon to finish.

I use a lot of yoghurt in hotcakes and pancakes, and more and more I use low-fat yoghurt at the end of cooking something like chicken, when I stir a few spoonfuls into the pan juices, to make a quick, non-fattening sauce. It will curdle if you overheat it, so stir it into the pan *off* the heat, and serve immediately.

Yoghurt, with two tablespoons (30 ml) bottled horseradish stirred into it, a teaspoon (five ml) of finely chopped or dried dill, a clove of garlic, chopped fine, and a teaspoon (five ml) of Worcestershire sauce, will transform plain boiled potatoes, particularly the little new ones.

Half-a-cup of yoghurt (125 ml), mixed with a teaspoon (five ml) of prepared mustard, one half-teaspoon (2.5 ml) each of dried tarragon, sugar, salt and a dash of cayenne pepper—this is a lovely sauce to eat with asparagus. I particularly like to make the dressing, cook the asparagus for five minutes, chill them both separately in the fridge (all afternoon or all day if you like) and then, just before supper toss them together, sprinkled with toasted sesame seeds.

Have a nice *slender* life.

Hazelnut and Chocolate Semifreddo

Ice cream without an ice cream maker.

1/2 cup/125 ml hazelnuts, chopped

2 oz/30 g chocolate, grated

1/4 cup/60 ml sugar

2 cups/500 ml whipped cream

2 egg whites

a splash of rum

1/3 cup/85 ml icing sugar

Fold the hazelnuts, chocolate and sugar into the whipped cream. Beat the egg whites until stiff and then fold into the hazelnut mixture. Gently fold in the rum and the icing sugar. Pour into dessert glasses or bowls and place in the freezer for 30 minutes, or until set. Serves 4.

Portuguese Rice Pudding (The Best Rice Pudding in the World)

This only works with arborio rice.

3 Tbsp/45 ml short-grain (arborio) rice

2 cups/500 ml milk

3 Tbsp/45 ml sugar

3 Tbsp/45 ml butter

zest of 1 orange, chopped

1 tsp/5 ml cinnamon

Preheat the oven to 250F (120C). Mix the rice, milk, sugar, butter and orange zest together in a bowl and pour the mixture into a greased baking dish. Bake for 2 hours. Sprinkle with cinnamon and serve hot or cold. Serves 2.

German Apple Cake

No vanilla? Use whiskey.

1 cup/250 ml butter, softened
1 cup/250 ml sugar
3 eggs
2 tsp/10 ml vanilla
a pinch of salt

2½ cups/625 ml flour
3 Tbsp/45 ml baking powder
2 apples, peeled, cored
 and sliced thin
additional sugar

Preheat oven to 350F (177C). Cream butter and sugar together, then stir in the eggs one at a time. Add the vanilla and mix until smooth. Add the flour, salt and baking powder and stir until the flour is just incorporated. Pour the batter into a greased 9"/22.5 cm round baking dish and arrange the apple slices on top. Sprinkle with a bit of sugar and bake for 40 to 50 minutes, or until done.

Easy Steamed Peach Pudding

1-14 oz/398 ml tin peach
 slices, drained
⅓ cup/85 ml sugar
1 cup/250 ml flour

2 tsp/10 ml baking powder
a pinch of salt
2 Tbsp/30 ml butter
½ cup/125 ml milk

Place the peaches in a buttered baking dish or in the middle of a large piece of buttered aluminium foil. Sprinkle them with sugar. Mix the flour, baking powder and salt together. Cut in the butter and add the milk. Stir until everything is incorporated and you have a thick dough. Spread the dough over the peaches and cover with foil. Place the baking dish or foil package in a steamer, cover and steam for 30 minutes. Serve with ice cream. Serves 4.

EGGS
IS
EASY

ggs *used* to come from chickens, nice warm brown eggs with a little bit of straw stuck on the shell, and fished out from under a nice warm chicken. Now they come ready laid in supermarket cartons, stacked as high and as tidy as an old-fashioned woodpile. You flip open the box, check for cracks—and the odd missing one—dump them in the cart and put them in the fridge, along with the leftovers, the yoghurt, the peanut butter and the jars of bugs, worms and grasshoppers that were meant for last week's Grade One show and tell.

Eggs just don't have the *dignity* they once did. The first food, the simplest food, the riddle of life, a magnificent engineering job—the egg has a lot of magic going for it on a lot of counts. It used to be the ultimate symbol of comfort. Wandering nomads couldn't keep chickens, but once they settled down, got a house, a well and something planted in the garden, they soon got hens. And, of course, they also got eggs.

Eggs meant *luxury*. They quickly learned that an egg in the bread dough made it rich, two eggs made it even richer, and three eggs turned it into cake. Suddenly, cooking had class. All the muffins we eat today, the angel food cakes, the *zabaglione* in fancy restaurants, the mayonnaise, the hollandaise, the Eggs Benedict—they're all *rich things*, things we remember with the especially satisfied pleasure that comes from something lasting and lingering on the tongue.

I think the ultimate luxury is comfort. When I was a small boy, my allowance came from the chickens that preferred to lay their eggs in the garden, rather than the henhouse. We lived in the country, in a damp and chilly house, and almost every day in winter we sniffed and coughed and our noses ran. There was no heat in the house, except for a small fireplace in the kitchen, and for a lot of years (any time is a long time when you're eight years old) I crawled into bed in my clothes (my socks, pants, shirt and sweater). Slowly, as the bed warmed up, I took them off and kept them with me all night until one by one it was time to put them on again, get out of bed, and draw, with my finger, rude words in the frost on the inside of my window.

When it got too bad (my nose like a running tap and a face like a Christmas reindeer) my mother would decide that school was off for the day. Tomorrow I would take a note, but today I would spend in bed. "Nice and comfortable" she would say, and for that day only I would have a hot water bottle. In actual fact it was a brick, warmed in the oven and wrapped in two towels, and for perhaps half-an-hour it did help, giving a little comfort and a little warmth. Most of the day I lay stiff as a plank and cold as a fish, my chest rubbed with goose grease mixed with camphorated oil, and I thought seriously (and as I remember, with some anticipation) of death. I hoped God would forget all the good things I'd done and remember only the bad, so that he would be sure to send me to Hell, where at least it was warm.

But three times a day, on those long days in bed, real comfort arrived. My mother, by no means the best cook, could boil an egg to perfection, not soft but not hard, and with it she would bring me toast cut into finger-wide strips. She cut the top off the egg, and sat there, looking as happy as if she herself had laid it, while I dipped the toast into the egg and sucked it—rich and golden and warm and every mouthful telling me that life and love went on forever and that tomorrow, just because of the magic of the egg, I would be better.

Recently, in a food trade magazine, I read about a man who had invented an egg slicer for restaurants. Because eggs are, well, *egg*-shaped, the size of each slice varies; some big, some small. The man had developed a system which separated the white from the yolk and somehow cooked them in stainless steel tubes which produced, as an end result, a completely uniform cylinder of hard-boiled egg which could then be sliced to produce slices of exactly the same size—truly a sad end for one of nature's really great miracles.

Not all eggs have come to this portion-controlled state, but the perfectly boiled (or perfectly scrambled, or perfectly poached) egg is not as easy to come by as it once was. And eggs have been getting a lot of unjustified bad press lately—cries and whispers, rumours and gossip about cholesterol, the bogeyman that nobody understands but everybody's scared of.

Most of these rumours are almost completely unfounded. The really big enemy of the circulatory system is saturated fats, and eggs have relatively little. Only a very few people with a serious cholesterol problem will be affected by eggs, but for the rest, not only is there no harm in an egg two or three times a week, there's also a lot of comfort, and a lot of joy. There's no cheaper way of getting either, and certainly nothing easier.

So let's start at the very beginning, with a boiled egg. Eggs like company, and two will cook better than one. You need a small saucepan, two eggs, cold water just to cover and a half-teaspoon (2.5 ml) of salt. Bring the water to a boil, and immediately turn off the heat. After four minutes you'll have the perfect soft-boiled egg, after five, medium, and 10 minutes later what the French call an *oeuf mollet*, which is an egg hard enough to peel but soft enough to mash. You peel and plunge into cold water and then keep them to use in salads, or with a tarragon-flavored mayonnaise. Cooking eggs this way ensures that there is no black ring between the yolk and the white. And eggs always peel easier under a running cold tap.

Now the perfect poached egg. You can buy an egg poacher (most people seem to get them as presents at showers) which is a set of little aluminum dishes set in a base. They will indeed produce a perfectly formed, clean-edged poached egg, usually as hard as a hockey puck. And just the sort of egg which is as comforting as a hockey puck.

But the really great poached egg (which will sit equally well on toast, or in a bed of mashed potatoes) requires a small to medium-size saucepan half-filled with water, a slotted spoon, a saucer and a teaspoon (five ml) of vinegar. Boil the water, add the vinegar, and crack an egg into a saucer. This is a business of perfection, not a production line. You have to fuss, so enjoy it—one egg at a time.

Stir the water in the saucepan carefully, conscientiously and vigorously until it's spinning fast, with a vortex in the middle like the water going down the bathtub hole. Now slide the egg directly into the centre of the spinning water, keeping the pan on the high heat. Let it come to rest, and the yolk will be in the middle, with the white all tucked up around it. Let it cook for three minutes (you don't have to time it, you'll see when it's just right) and take it out with the slotted spoon. Put it on the toast, sprinkle with a little pepper and a little salt, and carry it, triumphantly, to the table (or better still the bedside) of your best beloved. Better than *any* Valentine.

If you want to impress 20 or 30 people at a time with something like *Huevos Rancheros*, those spicy sauced eggs from Mexico, there is a way of making 40 poached eggs at one time, which will enable you to serve everybody at once, and have them all say how clever you are. Brunch, a Grey Cup party, or a fund-raising supper, this is dead easy.

First, make a spicy tomato sauce just as you would for spaghetti. Canned tomato sauce will do in a pinch, with some cayenne pepper, oregano and a bit of vinegar stirred in. Heat the oven to 325F (170C). Spread the sauce as deep as a sugar cube in a shallow pan, and make depressions (each big enough for an egg) about a hand's width apart (use the back of a spoon). Crack an egg into each depression, and bake until the whites are set and the yolks still soft (about 10 minutes). The eggs, complete with sauce, will come out easily one at a time with a spatula, and everybody, including you, will be delighted.

I like to make the sauce chunky and spicy, with red peppers and green peppers and finely chopped celery and a lot of oregano in it, and add a pinch of sugar along with the vinegar.

Then there's scrambled eggs, the most comforting of them all. The trick is to beat them very slightly, and cook them very lightly. Overdoing either the beating or the cooking will make them tough and dry. For two eggs just heat a tablespoon (15 ml) of butter in a medium-size frypan over medium heat. As soon as it's melted add a tablespoon (15 ml) of finely chopped onion and a sprinkle of pepper. Cook, stirring for one minute. Add a handful of mushrooms sliced thin, and a garlic clove, finely chopped.

Cook, stirring, just until it smells nutty. Add the lightly beaten (still stringy looking) eggs, stir gently two or three times, and cook, occasionally stirring (*always very gently*), until they are soft and still shiny looking. Salt to taste after they are cooked. Salt added at the beginning will make them tough.

These eggs, with brown toast, are the world's best cure-all for the sniffles, the sads, the occasional broken heart and anything else that ails you.

Almost Eggs Florentine with Easy Bechamel

"I love you." "Great, keep stirring." "Really..." "I know, let's eat."

1 tsp/5 ml oil
1/2 an onion, chopped
1 pkg frozen chopped spinach,
   thawed and drained, or
   1 bunch fresh
pepper
4 eggs

2 Tbsp/30 ml butter
2 Tbsp/30 ml flour
1 cup/250 ml milk
1/2 cup/125 ml cream
a pinch of nutmeg
a pinch of salt

Heat the oil in a frypan over medium heat. Add the onion and cook for 2 to 3 minutes. Add the spinach and pepper. Break the eggs onto a plate and gently slide the eggs onto the spinach. Cover and allow the eggs to poach for 5 minutes, or until the eggs are just setting. In the meantime, melt the butter in a saucepan over medium heat. Add the flour and stir into a paste. Add the milk slowly, whisking to make sure no lumps form. Continue whisking as you bring the mixture to a boil. After it boils, add the cream, nutmeg and salt. Bring to a boil again, pour over the poached eggs and serve. Serves 2.

Basic Omelette

A non-stick pan helps; just don't overcook.

3 eggs
1 Tbsp/15 ml water
a pinch of salt

a pinch of pepper
a dash of tabasco sauce
2 Tbsp/30 ml butter

In a large bowl, whisk all of the ingredients, except the butter, together until smooth. Heat a frypan over high heat, add the butter and then immediately after it has melted, add the egg mixture. Reduce the heat to medium and with a fork or spatula, stir the eggs in a circular motion for a minute or so, then let them cook for another minute. As soon as the eggs look almost cooked, loosen the edge of one side of the omelette and flip it towards the middle of the omelette. Slide onto a plate and eat immediately. Serves 2.

Sweet Pear Omelette

Breakfast, lunch or supper, an all day reputation maker.

2 Tbsp/30 ml butter
2 pears, peeled, cored
　and sliced
1 Tbsp/15 ml sugar

2 egg yolks
2 egg whites, beaten
　to a stiff peak
1 Tbsp/15 ml brandy

Melt the butter in a frypan over medium heat and add the pears and sugar. Let it cook 2 to 3 minutes. Fold the egg yolks into the egg whites and add to the frypan. Cook for 2 to 3 minutes, until the egg is set. Turn out onto a plate, sprinkle with a little more sugar and drizzle the brandy over top. Serves 2.

Pasta Frittata

Hot or cold–it's a great recipe for leftover pasta.

$1/4$ cup/60 ml butter
1 onion, chopped
1 green pepper, chopped
1 cup/250 ml mushrooms,
　sliced
6 eggs
1 cup/250 ml milk
1 cup/250 ml cheese, grated

a handful of fresh parsley,
　chopped
1 Tbsp/15 ml basil
salt and pepper
2 cups/500 ml leftover pasta
　(cooked)
2 Tbsp/30 ml parmesan

Preheat the oven to 375F (190C). Melt the butter in a frypan over medium heat and add the onion, green pepper and mushrooms. Cook for 2 to 3 minutes. In a large bowl, beat the eggs and milk, then stir in the cheese, herbs and seasonings. Add the pasta to the frypan and immediately pour the egg mixture over top. Cover and let it cook in the oven for 15 minutes, until the eggs are almost set, and the whole thing has puffed up. Sprinkle with parmesan and turn on the broiler. Leave the frittata under the broiler until the top is browned, about 2 minutes. Slice and serve. Serves 4.

Scrambled Eggs and Asparagus

A springtime seduction special.

2 Tbsp/30 ml butter	3 eggs
1 bunch thin, young	1 Tbsp/15 ml cream
asparagus, trimmed	salt and pepper
a pinch of salt	$1/2$ a red pepper, sliced thin

Melt 1 tablespoon/15 ml of the butter in a frypan and add the asparagus, sprinkle with salt and cook for 2 to 3 minutes. Remove the asparagus from the frypan and set aside. In a small bowl, beat the eggs and cream and season with salt and pepper. Melt the rest of the butter in the same frypan over a low heat and pour in the egg. Cook slowly, stirring all the time, until thick, creamy and cooked. Pour over the asparagus and decorate with red pepper. Serves 2.

Piselli A Torotino (Pea Cake)

2 Tbsp/30 ml olive oil	2 cups/500 ml cooked rice
1 onion, chopped	salt and pepper
1 clove garlic, chopped	3 eggs, beaten
2 cups/500 ml peas	3 Tbsp/45 ml parmesan
1 Tbsp/15 ml mint	

Preheat the oven to 400F (200C). Heat the oil in a frypan over high heat and add the onion and garlic. Cook 2 to 3 minutes, until softened. Stir in the peas, mint and rice and season. Remove from the heat after 1 minute and stir in the eggs and parmesan. Pour into a greased baking dish and bake for 20 to 25 minutes. Serves 2.

FISH, FENNEL AND FIGS

The fishing industry reckons that salmon may well be the chicken of the future. They'll be farmed, and marketed, in just about the same way as chickens are today. Obviously, the salmon aren't going to grow feathers and wings, and the fishermen aren't all going to sell their boats and live in the Fraser Valley, but there'll be a lot less salmon coming out of the deep sea on hooks and in nets. There are already salmon burgers in the supermarkets, and salmon sausages, and a whole lot of other salmon products in the pipeline. But just as there are free-range chickens today (if you've never tasted a free-range chicken then it's time you treated yourself) there will be wild salmon (and just like free-range chicken it will cost about twice as much). Wild salmon will be for the good restaurants and the fancy trade.

The big difference between fish and chicken (apart from the fins and the feathers) is cooking it. A chicken is *virtually* indestructible—even burned chicken tastes pretty good if you tell people it's Cajun style. Boil it, fry it, stew it or roast it. Chicken has a down-home finger lickin' good image inherited from the days of the early settlers, when the politicians promised luxury and security to voters—"*a chicken in every pot*".

Fish hasn't reached the stage of familiarity yet. Most of us are even a little scared of fish in the kitchen. A whole salmon is big enough to make an impression, and a salmon barbecue has a certain social clout, but very few people can be as casual with a piece of fish as they can with chicken. The truth of it is that fish is easier, quicker, and even today, probably cheaper, because there's so little waste.

There's no shortage of recipes for cooking fish, but far too many of them are based on the old meat approach. Stuffed salmon is invariably overcooked (because the stuffing takes so long). Three layers of foil may indeed stop it burning on the barbecue, but you might just as well take it with you into the sauna and wait while it steams. There is, in fact, a well known recipe for cooking salmon in the dishwasher; a whole salmon, wrapped in saran and two layers of foil, then laid on the top rack and given two complete economy cycles. It's a great way to show off your new dishwasher, but a terrible way to cook a salmon. It falls apart on the plate and it also *tastes* like the plate. But if soggy cardboard is your dream dinner…

There are some very simple basics to cooking fish. There is the worry about the smell of cooking fish. First of all, really fresh fish has hardly any smell. If it smells, or it looks wet and tired and half drowned, then don't buy it. There are two very simple ways of cutting down the cooking smell: 1. Light a candle and stand it on the kitchen counter (this also works for peeling onions if they make you cry), and 2. Fry thin slices of ginger in the oil before and during the cooking of the fish.

Fancy restaurants will offer *Truite a la meuniere*—which means simply trout as the miller would cook it. Flour mills in France were (and some still are) powered by water, by a stream which pushed the big wheel round and round. In the stream there were always trout; in the mill always flour. So the miller (or his kids) caught a couple of trout, dredged them in flour and threw them into a hot pan with a bit of butter. Very simple, very easy—if you have flour, and you have a frypan. You can use oil instead of butter but butter tastes *better*. What the millers didn't know, but you do, is a simple rule, invented some 30 years ago by the Department of Fisheries, and quoted in cookbooks all over the world as "The Canadian Rule".

It's easy. You lay the fish on its side (steaks, fillets, whole fish, just lay them all flat), and measure the thickness at the thickest part of the fish and you cook it, 10 minutes per inch (2.5 cm) of thickness. Frypan, hot oven, steamer or barbecue—salmon, cod, snapper or skate—whatever you choose, 10 minutes an inch. I personally think that's a *little* too much, and I suggest eight minutes, but start with 10 and you won't go wrong. (10 minutes an inch is the absolute maximum!)

This means that you can leave cooking the fish until just before you're ready to eat. You can get everything else ready—the salad, the dessert, the asparagus and even the fancy sauce if that's what you're going to do.

Flour sticks to fish, and makes a crispy skin on the outside, which seals in the juices and keeps it moist. Cornmeal won't stick, unless you first dip the fish in milk , but cornmeal will give it a crunchy texture which is very pleasant with white fishes like cod fillets or snapper. If you want extra flavour, mix pepper, salt and a little thyme (very French) into the flour, or a little sugar and red cayenne pepper, which will give it a hot and sweet crispiness (very Northern Chinese).

Salmon Teriyaki is easier than it sounds, and a lot cheaper to cook at home than to buy in a restaurant. Very few frypans are big enough for more than two salmon steaks, so if you're cooking for four then you will need two pans. Start with the pans cold, and pour in a puddle of oil about as big as the palm of your hand. Now pour soy sauce into the middle of the puddle, another puddle about as wide as a spice jar, and finally put a tablespoon (15 ml) of sugar in the centre of everything. Heat the pan over medium heat, stir it all together, and lay in the fish. Turn it over half way through the cooking (10 minutes an inch maximum!) and slide the fish about a bit in the melted sugar and soy mixture. It will be a coppery, sticky brown colour, which kids like the way it is, but I prefer with a squeeze of lemon juice and a sprinkle of hot red pepper. Salmon is very good cooked this way, but so are smelt, or squid or trout.

When buying salmon you should remember that the tail end of a salmon tastes better than the front end, the belly flaps are richer than any other meat on the fish and the cheeks are the most delicate; all of these parts are sold, just as chicken comes today, in breasts and thighs and legs and livers.

There is hardly any fish that is not improved by the use of a bit of ginger. Even the fancy French chefs are using it these days. They put a chunk of ginger in the garlic press and squeeze the juice over the fish, before cooking, or stir it into the pan juices after cooking to make a light sauce, or to be really fancy they then stir two or three tablespoons (30-45 ml) of heavy cream into the pan juices.

Lemon juice is another fail safe addition to any fish. All fish needs is a little salt to bring out the flavour, but it needs a lot less if you use lemon juice immediately before serving.

Dill, basil, or tarragon are interchangeable for cooking fish. Fresh or dried, and sprinkled over for the last two minutes of cooking, they all develop a delicate sweetness, they all go well with lemon and/or ginger. Best of all, if you have leftovers which you make into a salad the next day, their flavour doesn't deteriorate or get too strong, so they taste good cold.

Light cooking and quick cooking—that's really the essence of fish in the kitchen.

Salmon, codfish, skate and snapper look simple, and are simple. They don't need any complicated preparation.

Any one of them, poached in half-a-cup (125 ml) of milk, with a little pepper and salt, will make its own sauces. Sprinkled with chopped parsley it will look pretty. If you need something a little more sophisticated, the Italians make a *livornaise* sauce which is also quick and simple. A chopped onion, cooked four or five minutes in two tablespoons (30 ml) of olive oil, then add a chopped tomato, with a half-teaspoon (2.5 ml) of pepper and a half-teaspoon (2.5 ml) of salt. Stir it all well, cook four to five minutes, then add one tablespoon (15 ml) of vinegar, one teaspoon (five ml) of sugar, and one teaspoon (five ml) of oregano (thyme or marjoram will do just as well). Stir in a spoonful of capers, cook two more minutes and there you have a light, fresh, slightly spicy sauce which will also go well with pasta.

Don't let yourself be intimidated; fish is easy. Just *don't* overcook it.

Figs with Ricotta

If you can't find fresh figs, use pears or apples or oranges.

6 fresh figs	1 cup/250 ml ricotta or cottage cheese
icing sugar	cinnamon

Cut an x into the bottom of the figs and gently squeeze them so a bit of the flesh pops out. Roll each fig in a bit of icing sugar. Place the figs on a plate, top with dollops of ricotta, sprinkle with cinnamon and serve. Serves 2.

Fish with a Hazelnut Crust

2 Tbsp/30 ml oil	1/2 cup/125 ml hazelnuts,
2 fillets whitefish	chopped (or any other kind of nut)
1 egg, beaten	2 Tbsp/30 ml parsley,
zest and juice of 1 lemon	chopped

Heat the oil in a frypan over medium heat. Dredge the fish in the beaten egg and sprinkle with chopped hazelnuts. Add the fish to the frypan and cook for 3 minutes on each side, until the nuts are nice and toasted. Serve with a squeeze of lemon and some parsley and lemon zest sprinkled over top. Serves 2.

Pissaladiere

A different kind of pizza; a little fuss, but worth it.

3 Tbsp/45 ml olive oil
2 large onions, thinly sliced
2 cloves garlic, chopped
1 prepared pizza base or frozen
   bread dough, thawed
3 tomatoes, cut into wedges

1 tin anchovies
a bunch of black olives
1/4 cup/60 ml fresh basil or
   oregano, or 1 Tbsp/15 ml dried
salt and pepper
4 Tbsp/60 ml parmesan

Preheat the oven to 400F (200C). Heat the oil in a frypan over high heat and add the onions. Cook, covered, until soft and caramelized, about 6 minutes. Stir in the garlic and spread the mixture onto the pizza base. Arrange the tomatoes and anchovies over top and dot with olives. Sprinkle with basil, salt, pepper and parmesan, drizzle with a little more olive oil and bake for 20 to 25 minutes, or until the dough is cooked and the tomatoes have collapsed. Serves 4.

Pan-roasted Salmon with Sweet Peppers and Garlic

1 Tbsp/15 ml olive oil
2 red or yellow sweet peppers,
   chopped
3 cloves garlic, thinly sliced
2 salmon steaks
1/3 cup/85 ml white wine or apple juice

1/2 tsp/2.5 ml thyme
a pinch of cayenne
salt and pepper
parsley, chopped

Heat the oil in a frypan over high heat and add the peppers and garlic. Cook for 2 minutes, stirring constantly. Push the peppers to one side of the pan and lay the salmon beside them. Cook for 1 minute, flip and add wine. Sprinkle with thyme, cayenne, salt and pepper and spoon the peppers over the fish. Cover, reduce the heat and cook for 6 minutes. Sprinkle with parsley and serve. Serves 2.

Tunisian-spiced Baked Fish

Don't start it until the doorbell rings. Overcooking fish is what gave it a bad name.

1/4 cup/60 ml olive oil
2 cloves garlic, chopped
a pinch of cayenne
1 tsp/5 ml cumin seeds
1/2 tsp/2.5 ml ground coriander
1 1/2 cups/375 ml dried breadcrumbs

2 fillets whitefish
1 tomato, chopped
zest and juice of 1 lemon
a handful of fresh basil, chopped
salt and pepper

Preheat oven to 350F (177C). Heat the oil in a frypan over high heat. Add the garlic, spices and breadcrumbs and stir. Cook until the breadcrumbs are crisp and have absorbed all of the oil. Remove from heat. Place the fish skin side down in a greased baking dish. Lay the chopped tomato on top of the fish and sprinkle with lemon juice and zest, basil, salt and pepper. Cover the fish entirely with the breadcrumbs. Bake for 15 to 20 minutes. Serves 2.

Baked Parmesan Fennel

An appetizer straight from Milan–just don't use prepackaged supermarket Parmesan or you'll think it came straight from Sarnia.

2 Tbsp/30 ml dried breadcrumbs
2 Tbsp/30 ml grated
   parmesan cheese
1 clove garlic, chopped
1/2 tsp/2.5 ml rosemary

salt and pepper
2 fennel bulbs, trimmed
   and sliced lengthwise
1 egg, beaten
3 Tbsp/45 ml olive oil

Preheat the oven to 400F (200C). In a shallow bowl, mix together the breadcrumbs, parmesan, garlic, rosemary, salt and pepper. Dip the fennel slices first in the beaten egg and then in the breadcrumb mixture. Lay the fennel in a greased baking dish, drizzle with olive oil and bake for 15 to 20 minutes. Serves 4.

Fennel and Garlic

2 Tbsp/30 ml olive oil
1 fennel bulb, trimmed
 and quartered
1 red pepper, quartered

4 cloves garlic, chopped
salt and pepper
1/4 cup/60 ml orange juice

Heat the oil in a large frypan and add the fennel, red pepper and garlic. Sprinkle with salt and pepper and cook, covered for about 5 to 8 minutes, adding a little orange juice, if necessary—until the vegetables are cooked but slightly crisp. Serves 2.

Fennel and Orange Salad

No salt, no vinegar and almost no time at all.

1 fennel bulb, trimmed
 and thinly sliced
2 small oranges, peeled
 and sliced

pepper
1/2 cup/125 ml black olives
3 Tbsp/45 ml olive oil

Toss all the ingredients, except the oil, together. Drizzle the oil over top and serve. Serves 2.

Baked Figs

6 fresh figs
2 Tbsp/30 ml honey

zest and juice of 1 orange
a splash of whiskey or rum

Preheat the oven to 350F (177C). Zest the orange and set the zest aside. Prick the figs with a fork and place them in a baking dish. Mix together the honey, juice from the zested orange and whiskey and pour over the figs. Sprinkle the orange zest over top and bake for 20 to 25 minutes, or until the figs are soft. Serve warm or at room temperature. Serves 2.

GARLIC AND GINGER AND GRATERS

There are not many herbs and spices that can genuinely claim to change people's lives. Ginger—plain and ugly, knobby and khaki coloured —was first shown to me by a Cantonese restaurant guy, a mountain of it sliced thin, ready for the evening rush. The wontons were all stuffed (it was a social occasion, an afternoon visit; lunch was over, the customers all gone, the "Closed" sign on the door and the waiters were sitting around a table in the back, gossiping, dabbing ground pork into wonton skins with their fingers).

I was writing a magazine story on racehorse owners (11 of the waiters owned an elderly stallion called Lucky Prince, which to their and everybody else's surprise had come in *not* last, but *first* in a race).

So they talked about racing, and just like any 11 guys who owned a racehorse, they thought it was the beginning of a winning streak. They knew, they *knew*, they *always* had known and if they'd been cigar smokers we'd all have smoked cigars. But, we drank tea, and when the pork was all in the wontons we went into the kitchen to make more. Pork butt, green onions, a smidge of pepper and a handful of ginger, all chopped together with two cleavers on a big maple block. If you listen when you're in small Chinese restaurants, you will sometimes hear the two handed chop in the back, like the introduction to an old time jazz record.

I had a headache. They gave me ginger, not to eat, but to rub—one slice at the end of each middle finger—on my temples. With my eyes closed. And they all laughed. Pregnant women in China use ginger—one slice on each temple—when they feel sick. Morning sickness. So they laughed. But my headache went away.

A Javanese woman showed me how to make ginger tea (one of the world's truly great hangover cures), and I wrote my first cookbook—*Ginger Tea Makes Friends*. Since then, I don't think I could imagine life without ginger. With fish, with chicken, with vegetables, sliced thin and pickled in lemon juice and salt (it turns pink). I rub it on the inner wrists of the seasick on a boat; I fry it crisp with hot chili peppers and beef; I mix ginger tea with whiskey for the flu; I give my friends little white porcelain ginger graters for Christmas (most Japanese stores sell them, and they're also very good for grating garlic).

Buy your ginger as fresh and plump-skinned as you can find. Smell it slowly and inhale very deeply when you cut it, and who knows, your life might change. You might buy a racehorse and it might win a race. You might even write a cookbook.

Garlic Rotini

Make the sauce while it's cooking—much quicker than phoning for a pizza.

3 Tbsp/45 ml olive oil
2 cloves garlic, chopped
a handful of currants or raisins
a handful of pine nuts
1 Tbsp/15 ml dried chili flakes

$^1/_2$ tsp/2.5 ml salt
2 green onions, chopped
3 cups/750 ml cooked rotini,
   or spiral-shaped pasta

Heat the oil in a saucepan over medium heat. Add the garlic and cook for 2 to 3 minutes. Add the remaining ingredients, stir until well-combined and heated through, about 3 minutes. Serve immediately. Serves 2.

Simple Salmon and Ginger

10 minutes an inch of thickness for salmon—no matter how you cook it.

1 salmon steak
$^1/_2$ inch/1.25 cm fresh ginger,
   chopped fine

$^1/_2$ tsp/2.5 ml dried chili flakes
1 tsp/5 ml butter

Preheat the broiler. Place the salmon steak on a piece of foil in an oven-proof dish, and sprinkle it with the ginger and chili flakes. Dot with butter and broil for about 5 minutes, or until the fish is cooked. Serves 1.

Ginger Tea

4 cups/1 litre water
3 inches/7.5 cm fresh ginger,
   grated

$^1/_3$ cup/85 ml honey
1 whole lemon, uncut

Place ingredients in a saucepan and boil for 10 to 15 minutes. Remove the lemon and cool. Cut it in half and squeeze the juice into the tea. Strain and serve. Makes 4 cups/1 litre.

Mushrooms with Garlic and Parsley

Good bread, red wine and some travel brochures.

2 Tbsp/30 ml olive oil
1/4 onion, chopped
1/2 lb/225 g fresh mushrooms,
  quartered
2 cloves garlic, chopped
2 Tbsp/30 ml dried breadcrumbs
  or 1/4 cup/60 ml fresh

1/2 tsp/2.5 ml salt
1/2 tsp/2.5 ml pepper
juice of half-a-lemon
a handful of parsley,
  finely chopped

Heat the oil in a frypan over medium heat. Add the onion and mushrooms and cook for about 5 minutes, stirring occasionally. Add the garlic and breadcrumbs and cook for 3 minutes, stirring until well-combined. Add the remaining ingredients, mix together and serve immediately. Serves 2 as a side dish.

Black Ginger Cake

With coffee, with ice cream, in lunch boxes or watching the late movie.

1/4 cup/60 ml oil
1 egg
1/2 cup/125 ml sugar
1 cup/250 ml molasses
2/3 cup/170 ml hot strong coffee
1 1/2 tsp/7.5 ml baking powder

2 cups/500 ml flour
1 1/2 tsp/7.5 ml cinnamon
1 1/2 tsp/7.5 ml powdered ginger
1/2 tsp/2.5 ml salt
1/4 cup/60 ml fresh ginger, grated

Preheat oven to 350F (177C). Cream together the oil, egg and sugar then stir in the molasses and coffee. Add the remaining ingredients and stir until the flour is just combined. Pour the batter into a greased baking dish and bake for 30 minutes. Makes 1 9-inch/22.5 cm round cake.

Ginger Lemonade

For strawberry lemonade, add 1 cup/250 ml puréed strawberries with the lemon juice.

$^1\!/_3$ cup/85 ml honey

3 whole lemons, uncut

3 inches/7.5 cm fresh ginger,
   chopped

2 cups/500 ml boiling water

1 cup/250 ml cold water

Let the honey, lemons and ginger simmer in the boiling water for 10 to 15 minutes. Remove the lemons, let them cool a bit. Cut them in half and squeeze the juice into the hot water mixture. Pour through a fine strainer, add the cold water and serve over ice with lemon slices. Makes 3 cups/750 ml.

Tomato, Gin and Ginger Soup

A big hotel classic—fresh, bright, smooth and easy.

2 Tbsp/30 ml butter

2 tomatoes, chopped

3 green onions, chopped

2 inches/5 cm fresh ginger,
   chopped

1 tsp/5 ml salt

1 tsp/5 ml pepper

2 cups/500 ml water

$^3\!/_4$ cup/185 ml cream

3 Tbsp/45 ml gin

a handful of parsley,
   chopped

Melt the butter in a saucepan over medium heat. Add the tomatoes and green onions and cook for 2 to 3 minutes. Add the ginger, salt and pepper and let cook for 2 minutes. Dump the mixture into a food processor and whiz until smooth. Return the soup to the saucepan, add water and bring to a boil. Remove the soup from the heat, stir in the cream, gin and parsley and serve. Serves 2.

Garlic Vegetable Sauté

From a little bar in a little village without electricity in Greece.
We ate it with fresh mussels off the beach.

10 cloves garlic, unpeeled
3 Tbsp/45 ml olive oil
1 red pepper, sliced
1 green pepper, sliced
1 zucchini, sliced

salt and pepper
1 tsp/5 ml thyme
2 Tbsp/30 ml crumbled
   feta cheese

Preheat the oven to 300F (150C). Place the garlic on a baking sheet, drizzle with a bit of olive oil and roast in the oven for about half-an-hour. Heat the remaining oil in a large frypan and sauté the peppers and zucchini for 2 minutes. Pop the garlic out of their skins and stir into the vegetables. Season with salt, pepper and thyme and sprinkle with feta. Nice with noodles. Serves 2.

Spanish Prawns, Garlic and Chilis (Gambas al Ajillo)

In Spain, these are brought to the table covered with sliced bread to stop the oil from spitting and to mop up the juices.

1/2 cup/125 ml olive oil
2 red chilis, chopped
5 cloves garlic, chopped
1 lb/454 g prawns, peeled

1/4 cup/60 ml parsley, chopped
salt
1 lemon, cut into wedges
1 baguette, sliced thick

Heat the oil in a wok or a high-sided saucepan over medium-high heat. Add the chilis, cook for 1 to 2 minutes and then add the garlic and prawns, stirring constantly. Cook for 2 to 3 minutes, or until the prawns just turn pink. Stir in the parsley and salt. Place a slice of bread on top of the prawns and serve immediately with lemon wedges. Serves 2.

Garlic Mashed Potatoes

Sometimes I add a little chopped parsley.

4 medium-size potatoes,
   peeled and quartered
5 whole garlic cloves, peeled
1/4 cup/60 ml butter

1/4 cup/60 ml cream or milk
1/2 tsp/2.5 ml salt
1 tsp/5 ml pepper

Cook the potatoes and garlic until the potatoes are done. Drain, mash together with the butter, cream or milk, pepper and salt until fluffy. Serves 4.

Homemade Ginger Beer

3 cups/750 ml ginger tea (cooled)
1 cup/250 ml club soda or for sweet-tooths, 7-Up

Mix the soda with the tea, pour over ice and serve. Makes 4 cups/1 litre.

HOTCAKES AND HERBS

Just about *everybody* in the world eats some kind of pancake; some sort of fried mixture of flour and water, or flour and milk. Sometimes it's cornmeal instead of flour, sometimes there are eggs in it, sometimes butter, or oil, and sometimes chopped walnuts or (as in Southwestern France) ground chestnuts. In India they are baked in a very hot charcoal-burning oven—a *tandoor*—and called all manner of different names, like *naan*, and *chapatti* and sometimes they're stuffed with onions, ground meat or just chopped cilantro and a little bit of black pepper.

In China, they come to the table to be used as a shovel and a plate; something to wrap around M*u* S*hu* pork, thereby keeping the sauce off your shirt-front. That's not *really* any different to the tortillas of Mexico, or, if you want to go back seven or eight hundred years, to the "trencher" used in medieval England. "Trencherman" is a good old-fashioned word, still used to describe anybody who knows the way around a good dinner, but way back then, before dishwashers, before detergents and before hot water, it meant somebody who could mop up every last drop of gravy, whether it was on a shirt-front, a fancy dress, or, as the movie *Tom Jones* showed us, in a cleavage.

Mopping up is the *real* function of pancakes. *Maître d's* in fancy restaurants, who make *Cherries Jubilee* beside your table, use them to soak up the flaming booze, and kids at breakfast use them to mop up maple syrup.

In the construction camps that were my first introduction to Canada, we mopped up with hotcakes piled high. First, a hotcake and a lump of butter, then two or three fried eggs and another hotcake, topped with slices of bacon. This sounds like an unreasonable breakfast, but up there, up north, with the thermometer reading 20 *below*, eating was as necessary as diesel fuel in the trucks.

So, on top of the bacon went another hotcake, more butter, then sausages, another hotcake, some ham or scrambled eggs and finally, to finish off, the last hotcake and a couple more fried eggs. To complete this monumental structure, sometimes eight inches high, came a great golden flood of maple syrup, and occasionally, whipped cream or condensed milk. There was a moment of pride—like a kid with a sandcastle—before the fork went in. The eggs burst, the butter melted, the syrup puddled in with everything else and, in the same serious concentration as a Buddhist monk at prayers, the serious business of eating began.

You have the picture. But now, almost every time the gourmet press talks about pancakes, there seems to be an unspoken rule that copper sauté pans will be used, special—and expensive—flour will be purchased, fillings made two days before and sometimes the *crepes* themselves *pre-made*, separated by sheets of waxed paper, and frozen in sealed containers.

If you want to run a French restaurant, and charge your guests seven dollars a head for these *crepes*, then all this fuss is just fine, but there's a lot more pleasure to be gained from standing at the stove, cranking out *hotcakes* as fast as you can, with your guests lined up and asking for more.

So, let's start with simple hotcakes, not quite as plain as they might be, but undeniably the best hotcakes in the world. I get letters about these, and if you have literate friends, you might too. What you are definitely assured of getting are big smiles. Let the kids help with them (or whoever else happens to be around at breakfast time) and make it a social occasion.

So here we go. You need three eggs, one cup (250 ml) of flour, one six ounce(180 ml) container of plain yoghurt and one cup (250 ml) of milk. Beat the eggs until they're foamy, then beat in the flour and the yoghurt until they're smooth. Keep beating and add, one at a time: two tablespoons (30 ml) of sugar, one teaspoon (five ml) salt, two teaspoons (10 ml) of baking powder, one teaspoon (five ml) of baking soda, four tablespoons (60 ml) of vegetable oil or soft butter.

Let them stand for five to ten minutes; rub the bottom of a small frypan, (six inch non-sticks are wonderful for pancakes) with a piece of buttered paper, and pour in no more than a quarter inch (if they're too thick they turn to pudding in the middle). Cook over medium heat until bubbles appear all over the top, turn over and cook about a minute more, and then turn them out on to a plate. Rub the pan again, pour in another quarter inch, and you're in business.

Now some serious, grand-motherly advice. They'll keep warm in the oven, so you can all sit down at once, but they won't taste as good. Tasting good is important, because the better they taste, the more likely people will offer to do the dishes.

Don't use melted butter, just soft butter, because heated butter easily goes rancid. Use the best syrup you can find, because these are *special* hotcakes, and they're going to make your reputation and nobody wants their reputation tainted, *right*?

Two pans are twice as fast as one, and do even more for your image. And accept the fact that the first pancake—even in fancy restaurants—almost always sticks, overcooks, or in some way makes itself difficult. Give it to the dog, or the birds on the windowsill. Don't wash the pan when it sticks, just rub it off with the greased paper and start all over again. Medium heat means whatever works best with your pan. If it's too hot it will burn, so turn it down a notch. If it's not hot enough it will stick and go soggy, so turn it up.

Once you've got the cooking under control, you can start to be creative. Next time you make them, add a few blueberries, or some apple cut in small cubes and lightly fried in the four tablespoons of butter you're going to use anyway. Whatever you do, don't forget to tell everybody that these are *The Best Pancakes In The World*!

Now you should be ready for English-style pancakes, the thin, lacy, slightly crisp ones that the British wait all year for, and eat by the dozen, with lemon juice and sugar, on Shrove Tuesday.

You need a half-cup (125 ml) of flour, a good pinch of salt, one cup (250 ml), and maybe two or three tablespoons more (30-45 ml) of milk and two eggs. Stir the flour and salt together, beat the egg and milk together, then beat them into the flour until the mixture bubbles. Use a fork, an electric beater, a whisk—you choose. Butter a frypan (my grandma used lard, but butter tastes better), heat it over medium heat and pour in a very little batter. Tilt the pan quickly at all angles so that the batter spreads all over the bottom, cook until the bottom is light brown (when you turn it over, it will also look slightly crisp) then turn it and cook for a few seconds more. Put it on a plate, sprinkle it with sugar, fold it into three, sprinkle again with sugar and a little lemon juice and eat.

The trick is to make them as thin as possible while using the absolute minimum of batter. Non-stick pans are wonderful for these pancakes, which are normally made bigger than North American hotcakes. And don't worry, the first one may well stick, so don't be discouraged; making pancakes is *real* cooking.

Rosemary Potatoes

Rosemary and potatoes have a natural affinity.

4 potatoes, cut into pieces just too big for a mouthful	2 Tbsp/30 ml fresh rosemary or 1 1/2 tsp/7.5 ml dried
4 Tbsp/60 ml olive oil	2 Tbsp/30 ml parsley
4 cloves garlic	salt and pepper

Preheat oven to 400F (200C). Place the potatoes in a baking dish and place the remaining ingredients over top. Bake for 20 minutes, or until brown and crisp. Serves 2.

Fried Cilantro Stalks

Don't throw the stalks out! They have a wonderful nutty and licoricey flavour.

2 Tbsp/30 ml oil	3 cloves garlic, chopped
3 cups/750 ml cilantro stalks	1/2 cup/125 ml walnuts
1 bunch of watercress	salt and pepper
1 inch/2.5 cm fresh ginger, chopped	

Heat the oil in a wok over high heat. Add the remaining ingredients, toss and cook for 3 to 4 minutes. Season and serve. Serves 2 as a side dish.

Chicken Tarragon

2 boneless, skinless chicken
    breasts, cut into bite-size pieces
2 Tbsp/30 ml flour
2 Tbsp/30 ml oil
1 onion, chopped
1 cup/250 ml apple juice or white wine

$1/2$ cup/125 ml mushrooms,
    sliced
1 tsp/5 ml tarragon
3 Tbsp/45 ml sour cream
salt and pepper

Coat the chicken pieces in flour. Heat the oil in a frypan over medium heat. Add the chicken and cook, tossing occasionally, until browned. Add the onion and cook for 2 to 3 minutes. Add the apple juice, mushrooms and tarragon and simmer for 15 minutes, or until most of the liquid is gone. Stir in the sour cream, season and serve on a bed of rice. Serves 2.

Crepes

A lot easier than you think. Let them stand and drool while you cook them.

1 cup/250 ml flour
1 tsp/5 ml sugar
a pinch of salt
$1 1/2$ cups/375 ml milk
3 eggs

1 oz/30 ml brandy
2 Tbsp/30 ml melted butter
water
juice of 1 lemon

Mix all the dry ingredients and wet ingredients (except the water and lemon juice) together in separate bowls, then add the dry to the wet, slowly, mixing until very smooth. Thin it with water so that it pours like a thin cream. Melt some more butter in a frypan over medium heat, then coat the pan with a little batter, and cook for 1 to 2 minutes (don't flip!) gently, until done. Serve immediately with lemon juice and icing sugar sprinkled over top and roll them up. Makes about a dozen crepes.

Winter Pesto

You can use cilantro instead of basil when you're making any kind of pesto.

1 bunch cilantro
(Chinese parsley)
3 cloves garlic
3 Tbsp/45 ml parmesan

2 Tbsp/30 ml walnuts
3 Tbsp/45 ml olive oil
or peanut oil

Blend all of the ingredients except the oil together in a food processor or blender. With the machine running, add the olive oil and a little water, if necessary, until the mixture turns into a paste. Great on pasta or steamed new potatoes. Keeps in the fridge for a couple of weeks. Makes about 3/4 cup/185 ml.

Tomato and Tarragon Soup

Hot in winter, cold in summer.

3 Tbsp/45 ml oil
2 green onions, chopped
2 cloves garlic, chopped
5 tomatoes, chopped

a handful of fresh tarragon,
chopped, or 1 Tbsp/15 ml dried
1 1/2 cup/375 ml stock or water

Heat the oil in a saucepan over high heat. Add the green onions, garlic and tomatoes and cook for 2 minutes, stirring constantly. Reduce the heat to low and add the tarragon, cover and cook for 10 minutes. Add the stock and cook for 5 more minutes. Purée the soup in a food processor or blender. Season and serve. Serves 2

Green Beans with Feta and Mint

Springtime in Southern Italy.

2 Tbsp/30 ml olive oil
2 cups/500 ml green
   beans, trimmed
juice of half-a-lemon

1/4 cup/60 ml feta cheese,
   crumbled
a sprig of fresh mint,
   chopped

Heat the olive oil in a frypan over high heat. Add the green beans and cook, tossing, for 2 minutes, until the beans have just turned bright green. Remove from heat, sprinkle the remaining ingredients over top and serve. Serves 2.

Orange and Herb Infusion

Honey is better than sugar, loose tea is better than bags, and fresh herbs are always best. But even with store cupboard stuff, this is pretty good.

4 cups/1 litre boiling water
1/2 cup/125 ml sugar
a handful of fresh basil leaves
   or 1 sprig of fresh rosemary

2 tea bags
2 oranges, pierced
   all over with a fork

Pour the boiling water over the sugar, herbs and tea bags and stir until the sugar is dissolved. Remove the tea bags. Add the whole oranges and chill for 1 hour. Serve with fresh slices of orange. Makes 4 cups/1 litre.

IMPROVISATION

ooking is an art, and like painting or potting or making music, it's more a state of mind than anything else. It's fun to have a kitchen full of herbs and spices, and if you like to read in bed there's nothing better to send you to sleep, contented and happy, than a shelf full of cookbooks and a mind full of wonderful things you just might make one day.

But recipes alone aren't what cooking is all about, any more than paint-by-numbers is art, or lip-syncing is singing. *Really* good food, family food, or at least the sort of food that makes you feel like part of a family, is simple, easy and above all else, *spontaneous*. Most of it comes from "pinch" recipes handed down from one generation of illiterates to another, (a pinch of this, a pinch of that, and when you come back from milking the cows it should be done…).

The great joy of this kind of food is that it's foolproof and cheap. *Anybody* can make it, it's usually better the next day, and because it's nearly always cooked in one pot there's very few dishes to do. If you're having people to supper it doesn't matter if they're late, because another hour of cooking won't ruin it. If the kids don't get home when they should from the game, you don't have to get mad at them and spoil everybody's supper. If it needs a little more cooking, then give it a little more cooking. Let the appetites wait, but gently grow, fertilized by the smells coming from the pot. If you live alone you make as much as anybody with a family (simple cooking is always best in big batches). Freeze what you don't eat and resurrect it, complete with its original pleasure, whenever you need a little comfort.

This is not just one recipe—not just one special thing you have to learn to do perfectly. It's a way of *thinking* about food, accepting it, mucking about with it, playing with it and *enjoying* it. Which doesn't mean you have to put both hands in it like a two year old and rub it in your hair (although we all recognize and delight in the pure and absolute pleasure that kids get out of their dinners). What it *does* mean is savouring all there is in food; the smells, the colours, the flavours, the touches and the textures, all of which are essential parts of our appetites.

Microwaves are fine for some things, but they've been touted as being the answer to cooking everything, when in reality they're just a specialized tool. You can't cook a cake in a two-slice toaster, you can't make mayonnaise with a cheese grater and you can't mix bread dough with an egg beater. With a microwave you can't relax; you can't get the wonderful smells; you can't get the nice crisp outsides that come with slightly overbaked potatoes; you certainly can't get those wonderfully overdone, black and mahogany coloured corners on a roast that everybody (particularly the rare beef eaters) always want to get first pick at.

If all the schools stopped teaching "Cookies" in Home Economics, white sauces, and obscure technical details about flour, they could institute a whole new curriculum of simple, one-pot cooking. If Home Ec. were then made compulsory (for *everybody*: the jocks, the band, the eggheads and even the teachers) there would be a lot less concern about our diets. We could stop worrying about junk food and vitamin supplements and we could probably dump most of our concerns about weight, because good one-pot food is self-regulating—you're full before you've eaten too much.

When cool evenings begin to give way to the downright chilly ones, that's the ideal time to get out the big pot, and decide that you're going to be what the restaurant guides call "ethnic". The most favoured dish in Naples, in Southern Italy, is probably *pasta e fagioli*, a magnificently robust, heart-warming sort of soup. "Sort of" because it can be made solid enough for a fork or liquid enough for a spoon. The basic ingredients are very simple—pasta and beans—and there are more recipes for it than there are fish in the sea.

But, as I said right at the beginning, good, simple food is not recipe-dependent, and your own individual taste is the most important ingredient. The end product is yours, and yours alone, something to be proud of, and even more important, something to be remembered by. The Italians may well call this dish their own, but the Mexicans make a very similar one, so do the Lebanese, and so do the Greeks, who call it *fassolatha*.

You don't have to be Greek to cook Greek, and you don't really need anything more than most houses have in the fridge or the kitchen cupboard. An onion, of course, a good big one, some olive oil, three or four cloves of garlic, two cups (500 ml) of small white beans (or those small, pink and white striped beans called cranberry beans) a carrot, a stick or two of celery, some parsley, a bay leaf, some pasta (dried or fresh, egg or spinach or whatever you have) and a small can of tomato paste. That's it, anything else you want to add is optional. You don't need chicken stock or specially made vegetable stock, and you don't need a great deal of time because it cooks while you watch television or mow the lawn.

First of all, the beans. Soak them overnight in enough cold water to cover. If you're really in a hurry, then open a can, but rinse them well with two or three lots of cold water, to get rid of the tinny taste. Boil them the next day in their soaking water (and in the big pot) for five minutes, then drain the water, replace it with fresh, and simmer for an hour, with the bay leaf.

Chop the onion, the celery and the carrot (nothing wrong with a food processor, but don't overdo it or you'll have juice). Heat a frypan, add three tablespoons (45 ml) of olive oil, and fry the vegetables over medium heat for five minutes. Add the chopped garlic and fry another two minutes. Stir in a handful of chopped parsley, a good teaspoon (five ml) of ground pepper and enough salt to taste. Add the vegetables to the beans, stir in the can of tomato paste, bring it all to a simmer, add a good tablespoon (15 ml) of dried oregano (works better than fresh), put the lid on and let it cook slowly for anywhere from an hour to three hours. The longer it cooks the mushier it will get. 20 minutes before dinner, cook the pasta (elbow macaroni, rotini, penne—anything chunky) in boiling water for 15 minutes, drain it, stir it into the soup and cook it all together another five or 10 minutes. The starch in the beans, and the different starch in the pasta will co-operate, and together they will make a smooth silky, multi-dimensional sauce for everything else.

In some parts of the world they add diced potato for the last 30 minutes of cooking; in

China they add a cup of cooked rice; in Portugal they add spicy *chorizo* sausage chopped fine; in France they add smoked ham (or smoked duck legs in the South) and thyme instead of oregano; in Japan they use a seaweed stock instead of water; in Germany they add beer and caraway seeds, but basically it's always the same one-pot soup. It's *your* soup because you're the one who's improvised. And, as you watch it all disappear that's something to be proud of.

The gourmet bibles will tell you all the complicated things you need to make it: the special brands of beans, the imported ham, the sea salt and the peppercorns from Madagascar. D*on't* listen to them, and remember that this soup has been made in cast iron pots, in empty jam tins, and the ingredients have always been just what happened to be left over after a bad harvest, an invading army, a drought or just a long time without any money.

Grandma's Chicken Stew with Dumplings

October, a rainy Saturday night, and the prospective in-laws coming to supper.
You are good enough for her.

2 Tbsp/30 ml oil	1/2 an onion, chopped
6 boneless chicken thighs	1 tsp/5 ml pepper
1 clove garlic, chopped	2 Tbsp/30 ml fresh dill, chopped
1 carrot, chopped	salt
1 cup corn kernels, fresh or canned	1 cup/250 ml water

Dumplings:

1/2 cup/125 ml flour	1 egg yolk
a pinch of salt	1/2 cup/125 ml milk
1 tsp/5 ml baking powder	2 Tbsp/30 ml parsley, chopped

Heat the oil in a saucepan over high heat. Add the chicken and cook for 2 to 3 minutes on each side, until nicely browned. Add the garlic, vegetables and seasonings, toss and stir in the water. Bring to a boil, cover, lower the heat and let it simmer for 30 minutes. While the stew is simmering, make the dumplings. Mix all of the dumpling ingredients together to make a lumpy dough. When the stew has cooked for 30 minutes, drop tablespoons of the dough into the stew, cover and let simmer for another 10 minutes. Serves 4.

No-Cook Tomato Sauce

*Nothing quicker or easier. Sometimes I add anchovies, or cooked shrimp,
or even canned salmon.*

3 tomatoes

2 green onions

2 cloves garlic

$1/2$ cup/125 ml mint leaves

$1/4$ cup/60 ml olive oil

$1/2$ tsp/2.5 ml salt

$1/2$ tsp/2.5 ml pepper

a pinch of sugar

*Place all the ingredients in a food processor and whiz until well-combined.
Serve over hot pasta or rice. Makes about 4 cups/1 litre.*

Red Wine and Red Onion Soup

2 Tbsp/30 ml butter

4 red onions, chopped fine

3 cloves garlic, chopped fine

a sprig of thyme,
  or 2 tsp/10 ml dried

2 tomatoes, chopped

1 cup/250 ml red wine

6 cups/1.5 litres stock

salt and pepper

*Heat the butter in a large pot over high heat. Add the onions, garlic and thyme
and cook for 2 to 3 minutes, until the onions are tender. Add the tomatoes and cook
for 1 more minute. Add the wine and stock and bring to a boil. Reduce the heat and let
everything simmer for 10 minutes. Season and serve. Serves 4.*

Mushroom and Mussel Ragout

Fresh mussels, fresh mushrooms and that's about it.

1 Tbsp/15 ml butter
1 onion, chopped
2 cloves garlic, chopped
2 lbs/about 1 kg
   fresh mussels
1 cup/250 ml water
salt and pepper

$1/2$ tsp/2.5 ml thyme
1 cup/250 ml mushrooms,
   sliced
1 glass white wine
2 Tbsp/30 ml cream
2 Tbsp/30 ml parsley,
   chopped for garnish

Melt the butter over medium heat in a large pot. Add the onion and garlic. Cook for 2 minutes, then add the remaining ingredients, except for the cream and parsley. Turn the heat up high, bring the mixture to a boil, cover and let cook for 4 to 5 minutes, until the mussels open and the mushrooms are tender. Stir in the cream, sprinkle with parsley over top and serve. Serves 2.

West Indian Fish in Tomato-Banana Sauce

Nice, quick, sexy and simple. I've even made this with frozen fish.

2 fillets, snapper or
   any other white fish
flour
2 Tbsp/30 ml oil
1 tsp/5 ml cumin seeds
1 banana, sliced into
   $1/2$ inch/1.25 cm slices

2 tomatoes, chopped
a dash of tabasco sauce
salt and pepper
juice of 1 lemon or lime
a handful of cilantro,
   chopped

Dredge the fish fillets in the flour. Heat the oil in a frypan over high heat. Add the cumin seeds and fish, reduce the heat to medium and cook for 3 to 4 minutes. Flip the fish and add the banana, tomatoes and tabasco. Season, sprinkle with lemon juice and cook for 2 to 3 minutes more. Sprinkle with chopped cilantro and serve over rice. Serves 2.

Instant Marinated Mushrooms

1 large jar
a pinch of salt
1 cup/250 ml small mushrooms,
   left whole

1 tsp/5 ml dried mint
$^1/_2$ tsp/2.5 ml pepper
juice of 2 lemons

Place all of the ingredients in the jar, screw the lid on tight, and shake.
Serves 2 as an appetizer.

JAMBALAYA, JERK AND JUNIPER

J is for jackfruit and java and jaffa oranges and jerky and a whole lot of strange sausages called *jagdwurst* and *jaternice* and even *jesus*, *all* of which you can easily find if you happen to live in Germany or Czechoslovakia or up on the Swiss-French border. And J *can* be the most important letter in the culinary alphabet.

My favourite J is for juniper, which most people don't have on their spice racks. But, most good gins have juniper in them, and if you use gin for cooking, you get the juniper flavour.

So, the next time you cook a chicken breast, sprinkle it with paprika, fry it in butter over medium heat until it's within a couple of minutes of being done. Then turn the heat up to high and add a thinly sliced apple and a good splash of gin. Cook for two more minutes, sprinkle with lemon juice and tell everybody it's Juniper Chicken.

J is also for jicama, a very dull-looking tan-coloured South American vegetable which appears regularly nowadays in even the most conservative of supermarkets. Chinese markets also sell it, but they call it "yam beans", a strange name for something totally unlike either yams or beans. Inside the skin (which is easily peeled) is a crunchy, very juicy, white flesh, with the same bright new quality of taste you get with raw, fresh picked green peas.

All it needs is to be peeled, sliced very thin, sprinkled with lemon juice and a little ground cumin, and eaten immediately as a very refreshing (and very easy) salad. If you want to be fancy, and dazzle your vegetarian friends, mix the thinly sliced jicama with thinly sliced ripe papaya, and sprinkle with grapefruit juice and a pinch or two of curry powder. And, if you want to be macho, sprinkle the sliced jicama

with dried tarragon and toss it with a table-spoon (15 ml) of rye whiskey. J is also for juicy. Learn to look at fruits and vegetables with the same critical eye as grandmothers look at babies; they can sense immediately if they're healthy and well-filled and unfortunately (if you're not tolerant) juicy. Some people press fruits and vegetables to see if they're ripe, which is a great mistake, because after a dozen or so people have pressed *any* fruit it will feel ripe, when in fact it's just bruised.

Here's how you do it. Take fruits firmly in the palm of your hand and feel the weight. The heavy ones are usually the juiciest, the ripest and the freshest, since juice evaporates through the skin as fruit ages. Look at the skins of citrus fruits. The shiniest, smoothest skins (and those with the smallest pores) are the best and the juiciest.

J is for jam. If you're ever stuck for time (but you want to impress that special dinner guest) here's a dead easy sauce you can make in a real hurry!

Add a couple of tablespoons (30 ml) of *any* kind of jam to the frypan, sprinkle with cayenne pepper and add a small glass of red wine. Boil it quickly until it thickens, and drizzle it over chicken or salmon or even over tofu. Just don't tell anyone it's jam.

And J, of course, is also for *joyful*—plain, simple, joy being the most important ingredient in any kitchen. Let the kids start cooking as soon as they can make a mess. Let them make a mess, let yourself make a mess—you can always clean up later.

Sing a bit in the kitchen; play music; let your friends watch; try cooking with your arm around your beloved—there's a J in the middle of *enjoy*.

Almond Pine Nut Tarts

Twice a year? Rich, decadent and very easy.

1/2 cup/125 ml ground almonds
1/3 cup/85 ml sugar
2 eggs
1/2 cup/125 ml butter
1/2 tsp/2.5 ml vanilla
3 Tbsp/45 ml flour

1/2 tsp/2.5 ml baking powder
jam
12 3-inch/7.5 cm tart shells
1/2 cup/125 ml pine nuts
icing sugar

Preheat the oven to 350F (177C). Combine the almonds, sugar, eggs, butter and vanilla in a food processor and whiz until smooth. Add the flour and baking powder and whiz again briefly. Spread a thin layer of jam in the bottom of each tart. Fill the tarts with the almond mixture. Place the pine nuts on top and bake for 20 minutes. Serve sprinkled with icing sugar. Makes 12 small tarts.

Jerk Anything

Charmaine Crooks is the fastest woman in Canada. Her mother gave me this. It's the key to everyone's heart in Jamaica.

6 chilis
1/4 cup/60 ml vinegar
1 cup/250 ml water
4 Tbsp/60 ml oil
1 onion, chopped
4 garlic cloves
1 Tbsp/15 ml cumin

1 tsp/5 ml sugar
juice of 1 lime
salt and pepper
2 pork chops, skinless
    boneless chicken breasts
    or fillets of fish

Preheat the oven to 400F (200C). Combine all ingredients except the meat or fish and whiz in a food processor or blender until smooth. Place the meat or fish in an oven-proof dish. Pour the chili mixture over top and bake 15 to 20 minutes for pork or chicken, 10 to 15 minutes for fish, or until done. Serves 2.

Pork with Apricot Jam

Of course, if you've got fresh juicy apricots...but it was jam the first time I ate it.

3/4 lb/227 g pork tenderloin,
   sliced into finger-size medallions
flour
2 Tbsp/30 ml oil
zest and juice of 1 lemon
1 clove garlic, chopped

1/2 cup/125 ml apple cider or
   juice or white wine
a good pinch of cayenne
salt and pepper
2 Tbsp/30 ml apricot jam

Coat the pork slices in flour. Heat the oil in a frypan over high heat and add the pork. Cook for 2 minutes each side, then lower the heat to medium and add the lemon juice and zest, garlic, apple cider and seasonings. Cook for 8 to 10 minutes, until the pork is done, stir in the apricot jam and serve over rice. Serves 2.

Lamb Chops with Jalapeño Jelly

If you can't find jalapeño jelly, use red currant.

1 Tbsp/15 ml oil
6-8 lamb chops
1 Tbsp/15 ml rosemary

salt and pepper
3 Tbsp/45 ml jalapeño jelly

Heat the oil in a frypan over high heat. Add the lamb and sprinkle with rosemary, salt and pepper. Cook 4 minutes, flip, then cook 4 minutes more. Remove the lamb and add the jelly to the frypan. Heat until it becomes liquid, pour over the lamb chops and serve. Serves 2.

Chicken Jambalaya

New Orleans in a pot.

2 Tbsp/30 ml oil
8 chicken thighs
1 onion, chopped
1 green pepper, chopped
1 clove garlic, chopped
2 cups/500 ml rice
4 cloves

$1/2$ tsp/2.5 ml cayenne
1 tsp/5 ml thyme
1 Tbsp/15 ml chili powder
1 bay leaf
5 cups/1.25 litres stock or water
a handful of parsley, chopped

Heat the oil in a large pot or high-sided frypan. Add the chicken and cook over high heat until browned on all sides. Remove from frypan and set aside. Add the onion, green pepper and garlic to the frypan and cook over medium heat for 2 to 3 minutes. Add the remaining ingredients except for the stock and parsley, and cook for 3 minutes, until the rice is translucent. Stir in the stock and add the chicken to the frypan again. Bring to a boil, reduce the heat to low and let everything simmer for about 30 minutes, until most of the liquid has been absorbed and the rice is done. Sprinkle with parsley and serve. Serves 4.

SPECIAL K, KISSES AND KALE

Every North American family has a list of things the kids just won't eat. When the kids grow up, they dump some of the prejudices, but the rest they carry with them for life. They won't eat liver; they won't eat brussels sprouts; they won't eat meat with bones in it. Sometimes they won't eat perfectly innocent things, like peanut butter or raspberry jam, and sometimes they won't eat anything that just might have caraway seeds in it.

A lawyer I know, well respected for her reason and common sense, refuses to eat bread which has been sliced from the wrong end. What's the wrong end? "I can't explain", she says, "I just know." Her husband, a kind and tolerant man, won't even sit at the table if there's rice for dinner, and their kids, who find it all very funny, won't eat green beans ("They have worms.") or green apples ("They're not ripe").

There's no logic to *food prejudices*. Families seem to be born with a list, where they cross out a few things, add a few more and spend the rest of their lives telling everybody else about it.

I'm not *without* prejudices. The first time I ate dog I decided there wouldn't be a second time, and I felt the same way about eyeball soup in Japan (fish eyeballs are like little white marbles) as I did in Newfoundland. But I can't understand people who like chicken but won't eat rabbit, who like beef but shudder at horse. Reindeer obviously isn't going to be very popular at Christmas, and it's reasonable for teenagers to skip garlic for a first date. But most of our food phobias have as much reality as the monsters under the bed. We miss a lot by not being a bit more adventurous.

Vegetables are the worst victims of these prejudices. Green peas seem to be universally accepted (although I've met kids who won't eat them if they see them come out of the shell). There are children who like tomatoes, and an awful lot who like mushrooms, but I sometimes wonder how the produce departments in the supermarkets make any money at all when at least half the consumers (2.3 kids per family) seem to have either an active dislike or an equally active apathy for the nice fresh stuff in the bins.

It's not just the exotics which go ignored. *Bok Choy* or *Choy Sam* is a big jump for anybody raised on straight cabbage. Things like *jicama* (which looks like an unloved potato and tastes like a water chestnut) and even artichokes are understandably a problem for the meat-and-potato mindset developed by most Home Ec. teachers. The Canada Food Guide Rules don't mention *Gai Lan* or *Daikon*. *Basmati* rice isn't white, but it isn't quite brown, so it gets left out as well.

But there are utterly basic, simple things sitting there, just waiting to be used. Like Kale, full of flavour, full of vitamins, dark, rich bluey-green, curly-leafed and pretty enough to put in a vase. It gets passed over in favour of that pale and watery-white lettuce, which has neither flavour nor texture, and contains a little less nourishment than a large box of tissues.

Let's just look at this kale for a moment. It's crisp and sturdy, because it grows in the winter (I've got half my front garden planted with it), and it feeds half the population of Northern Europe with winter vitamins. It got itself a bad reputation in Canada during the depression of the Hungry Thirties, because it was cheap and readily available. Cheap food is almost always unpopular—oysters were once so plentiful that people could pick them up for free on the banks of the Thames and they were despised until they got scarce and therefore expensive; herring, which properly cooked, are infinitely better than trout, also suffer from their low price, until French restaurants make an expensive dish of them, smoked, de-boned and served with simple steamed potatoes.

Kale is indeed cheap. It grows like a weed, and has been around for billions of years, since the time of the dinosaurs, who ate lots of it. It is persistent and virtually indestructible; if you sprinkle a few kale seeds on any barren bit of ground, and give them no attention at all, you'll still have kale growing 10 years from now.

If you want a little magic for encouragement you can remember that the fairies in Ireland ride kale stalks behind the dark of the moon. If it's practicality you need, kale had a reputation as far back as the ancient Egyptians for being the only really effective hangover cure. And if it's romance that you seek, remember that kale contains large quantities of *phenylethylamine*, which is the chemical the brain secretes when you fall in love.

There's the sales pitch. Now you should try Kale and Potato Soup, a deeply satisfying, warming and vigorous soup, which is a standard in climates as far apart as Hungary and Portugal, Scotland and Northern France. It is the cheapest of all soups to make, and the ingredients, all simple, all easily available, combine into a surprising richness of flavour.

You will need a bunch of kale. Be ruthless when you buy vegetables—if you can't get them with the dew on, then make sure that they're fresh, firm and *healthy* looking. Kale should look like a party dress, crisp and frilly and shining. It should give you as much pleasure to buy as a bunch of flowers.

You will also need a good big onion, five, six *or* seven cloves of garlic, a dried red chili or a half-teaspoon (2.5 ml) of red chili flakes, one yellow pepper, a bay leaf, a teaspoon (five ml) of salt, some olive oil (or butter) and four or five medium-sized red potatoes (red potatoes are better in soups; they have more starch and they take longer to fall apart). You will also need some pepper (at the very end), and if you want to be fancy, sour cream, but I like this soup best when all the vegetables are plainly visible. It takes about an hour to cook, and with a loaf of the best bread you can find, makes a very satisfying supper for a family of four.

Now, the kale. Cut the leaves off the stems which run in a spine up the middle. Hold the leaves in a tight bunch and slice them crosswise about as thick as a telephone cord. Chop the onion into thumbnail-sized chunks, chop the garlic and yellow pepper and add them, with the bay leaf and the chili pepper, to three or four tablespoons (45-60 ml) of olive oil (or butter) which you've heated in the soup pot.

Cook it all for three or four minutes over medium heat, stirring frequently, while you cut the potatoes. Don't peel them, just cut them roughly into cubes a little smaller than sugar cubes, and as you finish each potato, dump it into the pot and stir it. Add a cup (250 ml) of water, put the lid on and cook for five minutes.

Stir in the chopped kale leaves and the salt, cover again and cook another five minutes. Now add seven cups (1.75 litres) of water, bring to the boil and simmer, covered, for 40 minutes. I also lay the kale stalks on top of everything for this last bit of cooking, because they are full of flavour but very tough. Just before serving I fish them out with a fork, and stir at least half-a-teaspoon (2.5 ml) of ground pepper into the soup. Garnish with a dollop of sour cream.

Now all of this sounds like a lot of fuss to make about a soup. But it's worth it—there is comfort in the pot, and pleasure. There is that peculiar satisfaction which comes from making something from almost nothing and there is also the joy of discovery—the same sort of joy that we see on the faces of little kids when they first see snow. And that's really what all learning is about—the dumping of prejudices.

Almost any fish—except sardines.

1-7 oz/196 g tin salmon, drained	1 Tbsp/15 ml parsley, chopped
1/2 a small onion, chopped	2 eggs
1 cup/250 ml cold mashed potatoes	1/2 cup/125 ml Special K, crushed
	1 Tbsp/15 ml oil

Mix all the ingredients except the oil together in a large bowl. Stir with a fork until well-combined. Heat the oil in a frypan over medium heat. Form the fish mixture into patties and place in the pan. Cook until brown and crusty, about 3 minutes on each side. Serves 2.

German Kale and Sausage

4 Tbsp/60 ml butter	salt and pepper
1 onion, chopped	1 bunch kale, chopped, stems discarded
4 smoked sausages, sliced finger-thick	

Melt the butter in a large saucepan over medium heat. Add the onion and cook for 2 to 3 minutes. Add the sausages, cook 5 minutes and sprinkle with salt and pepper. Add the kale to the saucepan, cover and let everything cook for 10 minutes. Once the kale wilts down, give it all a big stir and serve. Serves 4.

Soul Food Kale and Rice

You can use any greens—spinach, chinese broccoli—if you can't find kale.

1 Tbsp/15 ml oil
1 bunch kale, coarsely chopped,
  stems and all (keep stems and
  leaves separate)
1 bunch green onions, chopped
4 cups/1 litre water

1-14 oz/398 ml tin white beans,
  drained and rinsed
1/2 cup/125 ml rice
a dash of tabasco sauce
1 tsp/5 ml brown sugar
salt and pepper

Heat the oil in a large saucepan over high heat. Add the chopped stems of the kale, green onions, water, beans and rice. Bring to a boil and simmer over medium heat for 10 minutes. Stir in the tabasco, chopped kale leaves, brown sugar, salt and pepper. Simmer for 5 more minutes and serve. Serves 2.

Blackberry-Apple Crisp

Real country cooking.

1/2 cup/125 ml brown sugar
1/3 cup/85 ml Special K
1/3 cup/85 ml all-purpose flour
1/2 cup/125 ml butter,
  cut into pieces
1/2 cup/125 ml pecans

3 tsp/15 ml ground cinnamon
1/2 tsp/2.5 ml ground nutmeg
4 apples, peeled, cored and sliced
3/4 cup/185 ml blackberries or
  raspberries, fresh or frozen
1/4 cup/60 ml sugar

Preheat oven to 375F (190C). Mix the brown sugar, Special K, flour, butter, pecans, 2 teaspoons/10 ml of the cinnamon, and the nutmeg in a large bowl. Rub the mixture with your hands until lumpy. Toss the apples, blackberries, sugar and the remaining cinnamon together until the fruit is well coated. Pour the fruit into a greased baking dish. Sprinkle the topping over top and bake until the apples are cooked, and the topping is crisp, about 45 minutes. Serve warm or at room temperature, with or without ice cream or whipped cream. Serves 6.

LOVE, LEMONS AND LUXURY

Asparagus is the glamour vegetable which gets its picture in the social columns and on all the plates of the rich and the famous. And, like most of the rich and the famous, it is usually overdressed, in something rather complicated with a foreign name, because virtue, simple and unadorned, is never quite enough for our North American tastes. Nobody buys the base model car, the three-speed bike or the camera without the gizmos. We have this awful need to complicate things.

Asparagus, *very fresh asparagus*, is one of the world's great *luxuries*. China, Japan, most of Europe and America, North and South, all grow asparagus, and they all associate it with springtime, with all the wonderful things that come at the beginning of a year, bringing with them all those old-fashioned lovelies of words like "fecund" and "burgeoning" and "vernal". Even "pregnant" comes to have different meaning in springtime—the buds and the tips of what may well, in a month, be weeds but right now are beginnings with all the urgency and vitality of something brand new, just *growing*.

Those little bundles in the supermarket, skinny for the first month, plump for the next, green on the shaft and royally purple at the tip are our first and best vegetable, each spear a signpost to summer. We should learn to go past the well-travelled route of *Sauce Hollandaise*, and take some of the lesser known roads to pleasure and content.

First of all, plain butter—which doesn't mean margarine, or corn oil, or anything other than pure, cholesterol-laden lovely yellow butter—to melt over a plateful of asparagus; your *own* plateful of asparagus, and each person at the table fully supplied with asparagus and nothing else on a plate. No meat, no rice, no fancy concoctions of *nouvelle cuisine*, just the asparagus, very slightly undercooked (most cookbooks will say: still crisp, still slightly crunchy and brilliant green), with a salt shaker handy (just in case) and the quarter of a juicy lemon for the occasional drop.

This is asparagus at its purest and simplest. You must, of course, have chosen it carefully—the cut bottoms of the stalks should still be moist and should not have been strangled by an over-enthusiastic elastic band—and each of them should stand as straight and determined as kids in a school concert choir. If it doesn't fill you with joy and admiration, don't buy it. There will be more tomorrow.

First of all, a coffee pot, a garage sale special. Break the stalks where they break easily, about an inch (2.5 cm) from the bottom, and stand them, points up, in the coffee pot. Sprinkle a little salt over the tops, put two inches (five cm) of water in the bottom of the pot, and cook them lid on, for between four to eight minutes, depending on size. Pour off the water, take off the lid and there you have perfectly cooked asparagus, the tops steamed, the bottoms boiled, ready to melt the butter and to eat immediately.

If butter is not on your schedule, then use olive oil. Cook the asparagus in the coffee pot, put it on the plate, salt it a little, pepper it, drizzle it with olive oil and squeeze half-a-lemon over top. That's what the Italians do, with the best and most flavourful olive oil they have, and down South, where oranges grow—nice red streaked juicy oranges—they use orange juice instead of lemon juice. So can you.

If you don't have a coffee pot, or want something different, then a frypan will do. Any store which sells asparagus will also sell fresh ginger. Cut five or six thin slices of ginger, and fry them for a minute over medium-high heat in two tablespoons (30 ml) of oil (olive oil, peanut oil, safflower oil). Now lay in the asparagus stalks (snuggled up close and not more than two layers), sprinkle them with salt and carefully turn them in the hot oil so that each stalk is coated. Add two tablespoons (30 ml) of water, put the lid on, and cook for five minutes. This is basic Chinese asparagus. To make it Japanese, sprinkle the cooked asparagus with a few drops of sesame oil and a little lemon juice, or a teaspoon (five ml) of sesame seeds. To make it Korean, add a chopped clove of garlic and a pinch of red pepper to the oil (with the ginger) and sprinkle it with the sesame oil afterwards.

If you feel that you have to make a sauce, there are quicker and easier alternatives to Hollandaise. In Germany, they beat a teaspoon (five ml) of horseradish, the juice of a quarter-lemon, a teaspoon (five ml) of sugar, and a half-teaspoon (2.5 ml) of salt into a cup (250 ml) of lightly whipped whipping cream. In Southern France, they whip the cream thick with a half-teaspoon (2.5 ml) of curry powder, a little lemon juice and either tarragon or tarragon vinegar, then serve it with cold asparagus. In Northern Italy, while the asparagus is cooking, they melt a few tablespoons of butter in a pan, add four or five garlic cloves, chopped fine, and cook them for just one minute and turn off the heat. As soon as the asparagus goes on to the plate, add two tablespoons (30 ml) of finely chopped parsley to the butter, a pinch of salt and four or five pinches of ground pepper. This sauce also goes remarkably well with fresh green beans, dropped for five minutes into boiling water and immediately cooled under the cold tap, or with hot broccoli.

All of these dishes are easy, but if you want to put in 20 minutes of real cooking, and impress somebody, there is very little that is prettier than asparagus with mushrooms. You'll need two hard-boiled eggs, two tablespoons (30 ml) of butter, a small onion chopped fine, three tablespoons (45 ml) of finely chopped parsley, half-a-pound (227 grams) of fresh mushrooms sliced thin, plus a cup (250 ml) of whipping cream, a pinch of nutmeg, an egg yolk, a little salt and a little lemon juice.

Heat the butter over medium heat, add the onions and cook for two minutes. Add the parsley and the mushrooms and cook for another two minutes, stirring gently. Now put the asparagus on (or, rather, *in* the coffee pot). Add the cream, the nutmeg and the egg yolk to the mushrooms, and stir fairly vigorously, until the sauce thickens, for three or four minutes. Take it off the heat, add the salt and pepper and stir in a little lemon juice. As soon as the asparagus is cooked, serve it with the sauce over the butt end, leaving the spears to be surrounded by the quartered hard-boiled eggs. Very rich, very smooth, *very comforting*.

And finally, if you are a determined bachelor, equipped with nothing but a frypan, there is an appetizer I remember from Naples which can easily become enough for a main course. While the asparagus is cooking in the coffee pot, melt a good tablespoon (15 ml) of butter in a frypan and cook two eggs, sunnyside up. Put the asparagus on a plate and the eggs on the asparagus. Add a bit more butter to the frypan, stir in a teaspoon (five ml) of lemon juice, a half-teaspoon (2.5 ml) of wine vinegar and a tablespoon (15 ml) of capers. Stir for a minute, and pour over the eggs. Sprinkle with pepper, and a little Parmesan cheese.

Much quicker than sending out for a pizza...

Asparagus and Strawberries

Lust...

2 Tbsp/30 ml butter
1 bunch asparagus,
   trimmed and cut into
1 inch/2.5 cm pieces

1 small basket fresh
   strawberries, halved
juice of 1 lemon
salt and pepper

Melt the butter in a frypan over medium heat. Add the asparagus, toss and let cook 2 to 3 minutes. Sprinkle with salt and pepper, add the strawberries and lemon juice, toss and serve. Serves 2.

Chocolate-Dipped Strawberries

Bliss...

2 squares semi-sweet chocolate
2 cups/500 ml fresh strawberries
wax paper

$1/2$ cup/125 ml whipping cream
1 Tbsp/15 ml sugar

Melt the chocolate in a double boiler. Grab the strawberries by their stems and dip the bottom half of each strawberry into the melted chocolate, and set on a piece of wax paper to cool. Whip the cream to soft peaks, add the sugar and continue to whip the cream to stiff peaks. Serve the strawberries with the cream. Serves 2.

Love Apple Fusilli

The first tomatoes were bright yellow, and they were called Golden Apples. When the red ones evolved they often got called Love Apples—Cupid seems to love bright red.

2 Tbsp/30 ml oil
3 cloves garlic, chopped
2 tomatoes, chopped
3 sun-dried tomatoes,
   chopped

3 sprigs of basil or parsley,
   chopped
salt and pepper
3 cups/750 ml cooked fusilli
$1/2$ cup/125 ml buttermilk
parmesan cheese

Heat the oil in a frypan over high heat. Add the garlic and tomatoes and cook 2 to 3 minutes. Add the sun-dried tomatoes, basil, salt and pepper and cook a further 2 to 3 minutes. Stir in the pasta and buttermilk, let heat through and serve, sprinkled with parmesan. Serves 2.

Delhi-Style Gazpacho

Lovely bright coloured soup—to cool your passions?

3 heads broccoli, separated
   into sprigs
4 cloves garlic, peeled
$1/2$ a medium-size onion,
   chopped

4 cups/1 litre stock
zest and flesh of 1 lemon
salt
1 cup/250 ml yoghurt

Steam broccoli and garlic for 2 to 3 minutes, until the broccoli turns bright green. Place the broccoli and remaining ingredients, except the yoghurt, in a food processor and whiz together until smooth. Chill and serve with a dollop of yoghurt. Serves 4.

Poached Pears with Ginger and Lemon

Hot or cold, with or without ice cream.

2 pears, peeled and cored,
    but left whole
1/2 inch/1.25 fresh ginger,
    grated

1 cup/250 ml red wine
zest and juice of 1 lemon
a pinch of cinnamon
1/2 cup/125 ml sugar

*Place the pears in a small saucepan. Mix all of the remaining ingredients together and
pour over the pears. Cook, covered, over medium-low heat, turning pears occasionally,
for 20 to 25 minutes. Remove the pears, then boil down the syrup until thickish
to pour over the pears. Serve warm or cold. Serves 2.*

Zucchini "Pasta" with Lemon

I like this in the summer, when the zucchinis are deep green and gorgeous and crisp.

2 Tbsp/30 ml butter
1 red pepper, chopped
2 cloves garlic, chopped
1 zucchini, stripped into 'pasta'
    with a vegetable peeler

a sprig of fresh tarragon or
    1/2 tsp/2.5 ml dried
zest and juice of 1 lemon
1/2 cup/125 ml pine nuts,
    toasted

*Melt the butter in a frypan over medium heat and add the red pepper and garlic.
Cook 2 minutes, then add the zucchini strips, tarragon and lemon, and let it all
cook 3 minutes more. Sprinkle with pine nuts and serve. Serves 2.*

Lemon Curd

True love...on toast for breakfast.

5 egg yolks
1/2 cup/125 ml sugar

zest and juice of 2 lemons
2 Tbsp/30 ml butter

In a small saucepan over low heat, mix the egg yolks and sugar together, quickly stirring until the sugar is dissolved. Stir in the lemon juice and zest, increase the heat to medium and heat through, stirring constantly until the mixture thickens. Try not to let it boil. Add the butter, stir until melted, remove from heat and chill until ready for use. Makes about a cup/250 ml.

Simple Lemon Tart

Even truer...

1 9-inch/22.5 cm frozen pie shell, thawed
1 cup/250 ml lemon curd (see recipe above)
fresh fruit (raspberries and blueberries are great)

Place a piece of foil into the pie shell and fill it with rice or beans (this stops the pastry from puffing up when it bakes). Bake at 375F (190C) for 10 minutes. Remove the foil and beans, let the pie shell cool to room temperature and pour the lemon curd into the shell. Chill until just before serving, cover with fruit and serve. Makes one 9-inch/22.5 cm tart.

MEAT AND MUCHO MACHO MEALS

ambs and daffodils, dogs in rut and dandelions, they're all so sudden in springtime. The grass is so much greener and the most urban of back lanes sprout small wild flowers. Spring is a time of surprises, but, like birthday presents, not all of them are welcome.

Cold winds and runny noses, summer in the morning and winter at night. And rain, more times than sometimes. Wet and cold and calculatingly relentless rain. It runs down windows, it soaks into shoes and it takes the crease out of pants and destroys hundred dollar hairdos. Cops, hookers, people who walk to work and night-hunting cats all think twice when they're wet. Rain has no pity for the urban peasants; it locks them in behind their doors with the nineteen inch screen for friendship and a pizza for supper.

Spring is a time for comfort, and Saturdays the time of greatest need. In summer, there's the sun and in winter, because the stores all sell boots, we know what to expect. Fall has its memories, but spring is a teaser. You might get it and you might not…

There is no comfort like a stew in spring-time. Beef stew, pork stew, chicken stew and Irish stew; the cookbooks are full of stews, but very few people make them today. Stews take time, the long, slow, meditative and comforting cooking time that is *really* the main and most important ingredient.

A stew done in a microwave is no more comforting than a chest X-ray. A real stew, cooked slowly, is a state of enlightenment, a blessing, a commitment, a marriage. Not so much cooked as *gentled*, the separate flavours in the pot developing deep, subtle and complicated relationships, which the aroma laboratories can never hope to duplicate.

Most of us eat stews without ever thinking of the complicated processes that go on in the pot, and that's as it should be, because nobody wants to turn the dinner table into a research project. And it's very satisfying for the cook to know that what's happening isn't pure accident, and that all those grunts of appreciation (people don't grunt over *fine* dinners, just good dinners) are due to love and care and all sorts of other things that don't come in spice jars.

A stew is a great retreat from the world. Like bread-making, the putting together of stew takes very little work, but a great deal of quiet, comfortable *doing nothing*. This means that you can read a book, listen to the radio, do jigsaw puzzles, play with the kids, paint your toenails or just plain old nothing. But, nobody can accuse you of idleness because *you are making a stew*, and every half-hour or so you have to pick up the wooden spoon and give it a little stir.

There are secrets to stew making, which cookbooks seldom mention, because they are learned by just doing them. The first thing to accept is that the best stews are made with the cheapest cuts of meat. Old chickens make a better chicken stew than fryers. Beef tenderloin, which may be great on the barbecue, turns stringy in a stew pot. Shins, shanks, briskets and hocks, the inexpensive, strangely named, unusual cuts of meat are the ones to choose. And it helps, when you cook them, to forget the fancy names which the gourmets have stuck on them.

Like *osso buco* the famous Italian stew made of veal shanks. Italians don't eat veal as we know it, because it doesn't have much taste to start with, it doesn't have sinews to melt in the cooking (sinews make the sauce smooth and gelatinous) and somehow it doesn't develop the same round comfort as it cooks. When Italians make *osso buco* they use the shanks of baby beef, which most butchers will save or order for you, and which most supermarkets are delighted to get rid of.

So let's forget the name and the reputation of *osso buco*, and make a simple stew which just happens to have a remarkably fine taste, as well as being one stew which requires absolutely no stirring.

It's not a complicated process, and the end result is elegant enough for a dinner party (which is when you can use the fancy name). Shanks vary in size—some are as wide as a mandarin orange and some as grapefruits, but since the meat is cooked until it falls away from the bone it's not *too* difficult to see that Elizabeth and Philip get reasonably equal shares. One really nice thing about *osso buco* is the marrow in the centre of the bone, which is *voluptuousness* of such concentration that Queen Victoria (who was amused by nothing) considered it to be a prime aphrodisiac. She had the royal silversmiths develop a special spoon for fishing it out so that she could eat it cold on toast before summoning the royal gardener.

For six people you will need six pieces of veal shank, or baby beef shank, sawed crosswise two inches (five cm) thick, three tablespoons (45 ml) flour, three tablespoons (45 ml) oil and three tablespoons (45 ml) butter, one cup (250 ml) dry white wine (or unsweetened apple juice), one 14 oz can (398 ml) peeled tomatoes, salt and pepper, two cloves of garlic, chopped fine, six sprigs

of parsley, chopped fine, four anchovy fillets, chopped fine, the outside yellow rind of half-a-lemon, chopped fine.

Dust the shanks with flour, and in a big pot—large enough to hold them all lying flat—fry them in the oil over medium heat, turning occasionally to lightly brown all over. Add the butter and half the wine and cook for 15 minutes over low heat, turning once. Then add the tomatoes, the salt and pepper to taste. Cook, with the lid on, heat very low, for two hours. Check once or twice to see that there is enough liquid, in which case you add the rest of the wine.

The really important part of an *osso buco* is the *gremolada*, which is the lemon rind, the anchovies, the garlic and the parsley, all chopped well together with a sharp knife. I like to take the *osso buco* to the table, whip the lid off with a great perfumed flourish, sprinkle the *gremolada* over the shanks then stir it in to flavour everything for a couple of minutes while you fetch the rice.

Osso buco is traditionally eaten with rice, and for special occasions with a *risotto*. *Risotto* is too much work for a family dinner, so cook the rice as you normally do, but stir a teaspoon (five ml) of turmeric into the cooking water, which will turn it bright yellow. When it's cooked, sprinkle the rice with a handful of green onion tops, chopped fine, and you'll have a very decorative dinner, which took maybe 15 minutes of actual preparation, and no oven to clean afterwards.

Now, here's an all purpose stew, a big one-pot stew for the winter, which also, during the last 10 minutes, cooks the green vegetables—*all in the same pot*. For eight people you will need two pounds (one kg) of beef, pork or veal, cut from the shoulder and cubed into lumps as big as a walnut. Shoulder meat is not only the cheapest, but it's also the most flavourful.

Heat your stew pot over high heat, and add two tablespoons (30 ml) of vegetable oil or lard. If you put cold oil in a cold pot, then warm it up, the meat will stick; if you heat the pot *before* adding the oil, it won't stick. Cookbooks will tell you to brown the meat, but that's very difficult. Meat seldom browns—it just changes colour on the outside. So we'll *colour* it, which is best achieved by keeping the heat high and cooking the meat cubes in two batches. Add two large onions, sliced thin, stir well, put the lid on and leave them to simmer over low heat while you chop up two pounds (one kg) of mixed root vegetables—some carrots, turnips, leeks, kohlrabi, even parsnips (any or all of them).

Add the vegetables to the meat, stir once, and add four cups (one litre) of stock or water and a good teaspoon (five ml) of pepper. Bring to the boil, and simmer over very low heat for an hour. You may need to add a little more liquid halfway through the cooking.

Meanwhile, slice two large or four medium-sized potatoes into finger-thick rounds. Stir in a teaspoon (five ml) of thyme, lay the potatoes slices on top and cook for 10 minutes. Slice half a green cabbage the same thickness as the potatoes, lay it on the potatoes, sprinkle with a teaspoon (five ml) of salt and a teaspoon (five ml) of caraway seeds, then put the lid back on and cook another 15 minutes. All you need is good bread and eight healthy appetites.

You can tell them that it's a *pichelstein*—an old German recipe…

Beef and Guinness Stew

If you haven't got stout, any other dark beer will do.

1 lb/454 g stewing beef,
  cut into bite-size pieces
2 Tbsp/30 ml flour
2 Tbsp/30 ml butter
2 carrots, chopped
1 onion, chopped

1 bay leaf
1 cup/250 ml beef stock
1 bottle Guinness stout
  or any other dark beer
salt and pepper

Dredge the beef pieces in the flour. Melt the butter in a pot over medium heat. Add the beef and cook until it changes colour, about 5 minutes. Add the carrot, onion and bay leaf and cook for 3 minutes. Stir in the stock and stout, and bring to a boil. Reduce the heat and let everything simmer for 30 minutes, until it is slightly thickened. Season and serve. Serves 2.

Aunt Pamela's Sunday Pork Roast

1 3-4 lb/1.5-2 kg pork roast,
  boned and rolled
1/2 tsp/2.5 ml pepper
1 tsp/5 ml salt
1/2 tsp/2.5 ml cayenne

2 tsp/10 ml sugar
1 cup/250 ml apple juice
4 Tbsp/60 ml butter
2 tsp/10 ml dried rosemary or thyme
1/2 cup/125 ml stock

Preheat oven to 400F (200C). Rub the pork roast with pepper, salt, cayenne and sugar. Place it in an oven-proof dish and bake for 20 minutes. Pour the apple juice over top and reduce the heat of the oven to 300F (150C). Spread 2 tablespoons/30 ml of the butter and the herbs over the roast, then cook it for 30 minutes for each pound it weighs. Baste it every 20 minutes or so. When the roast is done, pull it out of the oven and let it sit for 15 minutes. In the meantime, you can make the gravy. Pour the pan juices into a small pot, add the stock and remaining butter and boil for 2 minutes, until it has thickened slightly. Serve with your favourite vegetables. Serves 4.

Lamb Shanks

Tom Jones ate these with his fingers.

2 Tbsp/30 ml oil
4 lamb shanks
1 onion, sliced
3 tomatoes, quartered
1/2 tsp/2.5 ml salt
1/2 tsp/2.5 ml pepper
1 tsp/5 ml thyme

1 bay leaf
juice of 1 lemon
1/2 cup/125 ml stock or wine
2 medium-size potatoes,
  peeled and sliced
  1/4 inch/.5 cm thick
2 Tbsp/30 ml parsley, chopped

Heat the oil in a pot over high heat. Add the lamb and cook 3 minutes, turning the shanks over so they brown on all sides. Add the onion and cook, stirring, for 3 more minutes. Stir in the tomatoes, salt, pepper, thyme, bay leaf, lemon and stock. Cover and let simmer for 40 minutes. Add the potatoes and let simmer 15 minutes more. Season and serve, sprinkled with parsley. Serves 4.

Corn and Black Bean Chili

"Macho" doesn't always mean meat...

2 Tbsp/30 ml oil
1 onion, chopped
4 cloves garlic, chopped
1 tsp/5 ml cumin
1 tsp/5 ml oregano
1 Tbsp/15 ml chili powder
1-14 oz/398 ml tin black beans,
  drained and rinsed
1-14 oz/398 ml tin tomatoes,
  or 3 fresh, chopped

1/2 cup/125 ml barley or rice
2 cups/500 ml stock or water
2 chilis, chopped
1 cup/250 ml corn kernels,
  canned, fresh or frozen
1 red pepper, diced
1 green pepper, diced
2 green onions, sliced thin
sour cream

Heat the oil in a large pot over high heat. Add the onion and garlic and cook for 2 minutes. Add the cumin, oregano and chili powder. Stir and add the beans, tomatoes, barley, stock and chilis. Bring to a boil and cook, covered, for 15 minutes. Add the corn and peppers and cook a further 5 minutes. Season and serve sprinkled with green onions and some sour cream on the side. Serves 4 to 6.

Pork and Celery, Greek-Style

2 Tbsp/30 ml oil
3/4 lb/340 g boneless pork,
  cubed
1/2 a leek, chopped
3 stalks celery (including
  leaves), chopped

2 cloves garlic, chopped
1/2 cup/125 ml white wine
1 cup/250 ml water
salt and pepper
juice of 1 lemon

Heat the oil in a saucepan over high heat. Add the pork and cook 2 minutes, stirring occasionally, until lightly browned all over. Add the leek, celery and garlic and cook for 2 minutes. Then add the wine, water, salt and pepper. Bring to a boil, reduce the heat, cover and let simmer 20 minutes. Stir in the lemon juice and serve. Goes well with potatoes or rice. Serves 2.

Lamb Meatballs with Yoghurt-Cumin Sauce

Persian delights, these...

1 lb/454 g ground lamb
1 clove garlic, chopped
1 onion, chopped
a handful of cilantro
1 thick slice white bread
$1/2$ tsp/2.5 ml cinnamon

salt and pepper
1 Tbsp/15 ml oil
1 cup/250 ml plain yoghurt
$1/2$ tsp/2.5 ml cumin seeds
    or ground cumin

Mix all of the ingredients except the oil, yoghurt and cumin in a food processor until well-blended. Take one tablespoon/15 ml of the mixture into your hands and roll it into a ping-pong sized ball. Set aside and repeat until you have used up all of the mixture. Toast the cumin in a frypan over high heat for 30 seconds, or until you can smell it. Stir it into the yoghurt and set the yoghurt aside. In the same frypan, heat the oil, add the meatballs and cook over medium heat until browned on all sides, about 8 minutes. Serve with the yoghurt as a dipping sauce. Serves 4 as an appetizer.

NOODLES AND THE NEXT BEST THING

Not so long ago there were *no* noodles in North America. There was spaghetti, and when it didn't come in a can it was served along with an old and stupid joke about throwing it at the wall to see if it stuck and then you knew it was done. There was really only one kind of sauce and it was always a family recipe filled with secret ingredients handed down from an Italian grandma (the McTavishes, the Wodzinskis and even the Johnsons all had Italian ancestors when it came to spaghetti night). The sauce took hours to make—sometimes *days*—and there were little meatballs floating in it that looked just like cannon balls made for toy soldiers. Wine came in bottles with straw wrapped round the bottom, garlic bread was obligatory, and dessert was invariably a cheesecake made from the recipe on the back of the graham wafer box.

Noodles could also be found in chicken noodle soup; *nasty* little bits of skinny, soft and slimy stuff, looking like a worm farm in a bowl. This came from a can, unless it was found in a cellophane packet called *Soup-In-a-Mug*. Hospitals, jails, kindergartens and coffee shops in industrial parks bought chicken noodle soup by the ton. But, the only way I ever found it to be at *all* tolerable was to bring it out under the cover of dark; during late night clam-digging parties or fireworks parties and serving it with two ounces of rye whiskey in every mug.

Then came *pasta*! And, not just spaghetti, but *rigatoni* and *farfalle* and *rotini* and *orecchiette; angel hair* pasta and *linguini* from hand-cranked pasta machines (meatballs were dumped in favour of exotic sauces like *pesto* and *arrabiata* and *puttanesca*). Nobody was anybody unless they could say *tagliatelle* or *mafaldine*, and the pepper mill manufacturers made a fortune, because none of it meant anything unless it had fresh ground pepper added at the last minute.

Finally came noodles—*real* noodles—mostly from the Orient. Fat noodles like Japanese *udon*, skinny noodles like *ramen*, egg noodles, cellophane noodles, buckwheat noodles and rice noodles. Little restaurants suddenly opened up all over, selling nothing but noodles, in soup, or fried or steamed, and then along came peanut sauce and spicy sauce and black bean sauce and hot noodles and cold noodles like Japanese *zaru soba*.

They were the improviser's dream, once we realized that they were *interchangeable*. Fat noodles took longer to cook than thin ones, and some of the really skinny ones cooked by just being dropped into boiling water for one minute. Meat, vegetables, soups, salads; even as dessert when mixed with fat golden raisins briefly fried in butter, and the whole buttery dish lightly sprinkled with sugar. We suddenly discovered that good Jewish *bubbas* had been doing all of these things for years, making *kugel* and even stuffing turkeys with noodles.

M-m-m-m…Maybe it *wasn't* Marco Polo who brought pasta back from his trip to China?

Fettucine alla Carrettiera

4 slices bacon, chopped
1-7 oz/196 g tin tuna
2 cups/500 ml sliced mushrooms
2 cloves garlic, chopped
salt and pepper

1 Tbsp/15 ml oregano
1/2 cup/125 ml white wine
4 cups/1 litre cooked fettucine
a handful of black olives
a handful of parsley, chopped

Heat the bacon in a frypan over high heat. When it is translucent, add the tuna, mushrooms, garlic and seasonings. Stir well and pour in the wine. Heat through and toss with the pasta and olives, garnish with chopped parsley and serve immediately. Serves 4.

Middle Eastern Spaghetti

1 lb/454 g spaghetti
2 cups/500 ml yoghurt
3 cloves garlic, chopped
1 cup/250 ml feta cheese, crumbled

a handful of parsley, chopped
2 Tbsp/30 ml olive oil
a handful of mixed olives
zest and juice of half-a-lemon

Cook the spaghetti and drain. Meanwhile, mix the yoghurt, garlic, feta and parsley together. Drizzle the oil and lemon juice over the spaghetti, pour the yoghurt mixture over top, toss well and sprinkle with olives and lemon zest. Serves 4.

Hot Pepper and Sultana Pasta

3 Tbsp/45 ml olive oil
1/2 tsp/2.5 ml cayenne
3 cloves garlic, chopped
a handful of parsley, chopped
4 anchovy fillets

1/4 cup/60 ml walnuts, toasted
1/2 cup/125 ml sultanas
4 cups/1 litre cooked pasta
salt and pepper

Heat the oil in a frypan over high heat. Add the cayenne, garlic, parsley, anchovies, walnuts and sultanas. Cook 2 minutes, stirring constantly and mashing the anchovies. Stir in the pasta, heat through, season and serve. Serves 2.

Linguini with Clams

The sauce takes much less time than the pasta.

2 Tbsp/30 ml oil
2 cloves garlic, chopped
1 red pepper, chopped
1-14 oz/398 ml tin clams,
   drained, or
   1 lb/454 g fresh clams

a splash of white wine or
   apple juice
1 bunch spinach, trimmed,
   (or frozen, chopped)
4 cups/1 litre cooked linguini,
   drained

Put the pasta on to cook. Heat the oil in a saucepan over high heat. Add the garlic and red pepper and cook for 2 minutes. Add the clams, wine and spinach, stir and cover. Cook a further 3 to 4 minutes, until the clams open. Toss the clam mixture with the cooked linguini and serve. Serves 2.

Real Mac and Cheese

If it ain't broke, don't fix it.

2 Tbsp/30 ml butter
2 Tbsp/30 ml flour
2 cups/500 ml milk
2 cups/500 ml grated cheddar
   or Jack cheese

$\frac{1}{2}$ tsp/2.5 ml dry mustard
a pinch of paprika
4 cups/1 litre cooked macaroni

Preheat the oven to 350F (177C). Melt the butter in a saucepan over medium heat. Stir in the flour to make a paste, and remove the pan from the heat. Stir in the milk, a bit at a time so it doesn't get lumpy. Return the pan to the heat and keep stirring until the mixture comes to a boil and has thickened. Stir in the cheese, mustard and paprika, reduce heat to low and keep stirring until the cheese has melted. Pour the sauce over the cooked macaroni and place the mixture into a greased baking dish. Bake for 20 to 25 minutes, or until bubbly and lightly browned. Serves 2.

Szechuan Noodles

Hot noodles in winter, cold noodles in summer.

1/2 tsp/2.5 ml pepper
1/2 tsp/2.5 ml cayenne
a pinch of fennel or
   anise seeds
1/2 inch/1.25 cm fresh
   ginger, grated
2 cloves garlic, chopped

1/3 cup/85 ml soy sauce
2 Tbsp/30 ml vinegar
4 tsp/20 ml sugar
3 Tbsp/45 ml sesame oil
2 green onions, chopped
4 cups/1 litre cooked Chinese
   noodles, or linguini

Combine all of the ingredients except the noodles in a bowl and stir until the sugar is dissolved. Pour the mixture over noodles and serve. Serves 2.

Vegetarian Goulash

The paprika gives it the colour, the cheese gives it the texture.

2 Tbsp/30 ml oil
1 onion, chopped
2 cloves garlic, chopped
1 green pepper, chopped
2 tomatoes, chopped
1/2 cup/125 ml tomato juice
1 cup/250 ml sour cream

2 tsp/10 ml Hungarian paprika
1 lb/454 g egg noodles,
   cooked and drained
salt and pepper
3/4 cup/185 ml grated
   parmesan or cheddar cheese

Preheat the oven to 350F (177C). Heat the oil in a frypan over high heat. Add the onion, garlic, green pepper and tomatoes. Cook for 2 minutes. Stir in the remaining ingredients except for the cheese, season, and pour the mixture into a greased baking dish. Bake for 20 to 25 minutes, sprinkle with cheese and bake for 5 minutes more. Serves 4.

THE STORY OF O

Food must be an advertising agency's nightmare, because the essence of good food is its simplicity. Mushrooms are marvellous, salmon's simply super, butter's best and garlic is good for you. These are all fine, true and accurate slogans—all of them describing basic, simple products. But the problem with simplicity is running out of words when all the good ones (the fine true ones and the simple ones) are taken.

One of these days an agency is going to be hired to do something for onions. The slogans will appear on TV—"*Onions are Optional*" or even "*Onions are Orgasmic*". The real truth is that onions are *extra-ordinary*.

Without onions there is virtually no cooking. The slicing, dicing and chopping of an onion is one of the first things an apprentice learns in the kitchen, and every day that dinner leaves *any* kitchen, there will be more onions. French, German, Chinese, Hungarian or Ethiopian; everybody uses onions, and has done so all over the world ever since—and before—history began.

There's an old Turkish legend which says that when Satan was turfed out of Heaven, garlic sprouted where he put down his left foot and onions from his right. The first written records, from 2500 BC, tell of the gods ploughing up the gardens of the governor of Babylon because he had planted onions in their best fields. Onions, garlic and shallots recur constantly in the literature of sociology, anthropology, folklore, religion, business and international trade.

The first formal code of law in the world, *The Code of Hammurabi*, stipulated that the poor and the needy should get a monthly ration of bread and onions; at the same time, onions were being grown as a particularly special delicacy in the gardens of kings.

But, despite this, there is a long standing set of prejudices against onions. The early guilds of fruit and vegetable sellers refused to let the onion-mongers into their membership, and forced them to start their own association. Even today, in comic strips and cartoons, the onion is almost universally recognized as a symbol of social undesirability and foreign nastiness. It's more than a little ridiculous—a reverse form of snobbery—because *you just can't cook without onions!*

Fancy names, however, always make things acceptable to snobs. Onion Soup is somehow different when it's called "*Soupe a l'oignon, façon les Halles*". Beef Stew with Onions is a simple family supper, but call it *Carbonnades a la Flamande*, and it stands in line for rave reviews at the Gourmet Supper Club. My mother makes what she calls "my onion dish" which we always ate either with lamb chops and fried mushrooms, or with turkey at Christmas. She was quite surprised to find, at a fancy country hotel, that it was really called *Purée Soubise a l'Italienne*; now she's ashamed to make it in case it isn't "proper".

Here's the recipe, and you can call it what *you* like, but remember that kids, the most conservative of eaters, invariably prefer simple names like "that rice thing you make".

You will need one or two very large onions, some butter, a little whipping cream, two cups (500 ml) of Italian rice (*arborio* rice, which most supermarkets sell nowadays), four cups (one litre) of chicken stock, pepper, salt and a pinch of sugar.

Chop the onion into small pieces, and stir two tablespoons (30 ml) of butter into a saucepan over low to medium heat. As soon as the onion glistens a little, cover the pan and let it cook (still over low to medium heat) for 15 minutes. Stir in a good teaspoon (five ml) of black pepper, then all the rice. Stir the rice to coat it with the onions and butter, then add four cups (one litre) of stock and the pinch of sugar. Bring to the boil, lower to simmer, and let it cook, uncovered, until the rice is very tender (a grain should almost break up when rubbed between finger and thumb). This should take about 30 to 35 minutes, stirring every five.

If you want to be *very* professional you can rub it all through a sieve, or give it a couple of bursts in the food processor. I like it a little knobbly, so I leave it when it comes out of the pan. It can be eaten immediately, but it will improve, kept refrigerated, for a couple of days. Reheat with two tablespoons (30 ml) melted butter, six tablespoons (90 ml) of whipping cream and salt to taste. Decorate with a little chopped parsley. (If it's Christmas, stir in a dozen or two of boiled, skinned and coarsely chopped chestnuts. Much better than mashed potatoes.)

Now for something *really* simple. Next time you cook a roast, or have the oven on for an hour or so, take one medium-sized brown onion for each person. Don't peel it, don't take the skin off; just brush it lightly with a little oil, using a paper towel. Place them in a baking tin (or just alongside the roast) and let them cook at 350F (177C) for an hour. Serve as is, the skin crisp and papery, and the inside *incredibly* sweet. I have eaten a whole supper of onions cooked like this in Northern France—three or four onions apiece, lots of bread and tumblers of cheap red wine, the insides of the onions daubed with butter and occasionally dipped into the wine.

This is one of the best simple dishes in the world, something cooked originally at the side of a wood fire, or on a stick turned slowly in the flames. In Burgundy, where they seem to grow smaller onions, it's been developed into something just a little more complicated but an awful lot richer.

For each person you'll need three or four small onions, about the size of a walnut, or some pickling onions. Whatever you use, the onions should all be of the same size. Boil a pot of water, and drop in the onions for no more than a minute. Take them out with a slotted spoon and dump them immediately into cold water; the outer skins will easily rub off.

Put the peeled onions into a pan large enough to hold them all in a single layer. Cover them with cold water, and add two teaspoons (10 ml) of sugar, a good pinch of salt and a good big heaping tablespoon (15 ml) of butter. Bring the whole pot to a good rolling boil, stir the onions with a wooden spoon to coat them, and then turn down the heat enough to keep it just bubbling. Sprinkle a healthy dose of black pepper over everything, stir in a tablespoon (15 ml) of vinegar, and watch everything turn to a rich brown syrup in the bottom of the pan. Gently shake the onions (you may have to turn them over carefully) so that they get glazed *all* over; watch the heat very carefully for the last couple of minutes so that they don't burn. They are wonderful hot, but they're also very good cold. French chefs serve them with braised lettuce; they use them to liven up stews that have somehow become tasteless and they use them as garnishes for all manner of simple dishes, including brussels sprouts or plain boiled potatoes.

Finally, one more recipe that's *real* easy. Slowly fry three or four large onions, sliced thin, in two or three tablespoons (30-45 ml) of vegetable oil. Stir for two or three minutes, sprinkle them well with pepper, stir in a teaspoon (five ml) of caraway seeds, put the lid on and let them sweat for 10 minutes. Stir in a teaspoon (five ml) of vinegar, sprinkle with salt. Serve them with hamburgers, hot dogs, or plain fried sausages. Put them under a piece of simply cooked fish, or under stir-fried tofu, or alongside grilled chicken.

There's just no end to all the things onions can do. And, best of all, they're usually around 30 cents a pound...

Venetian Orange and Onion Salad

Get nice juicy oranges.

3 oranges, peeled and sliced thin	olive oil
1 red onion, sliced thin	salt and pepper

Toss the oranges and onions together, drizzle the oil over top, sprinkle with a bit of salt and pepper and serve. Serves 2.

Lamb and Oranges

2 Tbsp/30 ml oil	1 orange, cut into eighths,
1 small onion, chopped	skin left on
1 clove garlic, chopped	a sprig of fresh mint,
6 lamb chops	chopped

Heat the oil in a large frypan over high heat. Add the onion and garlic and cook 2 minutes. Shove the onion mixture to one side of the pan and add the lamb chops. Cook for 2 minutes, turn the chops over, cook another 2 minutes, then squeeze the oranges over the lamb and add them to the pan with the mint. Cover and let cook 5 minutes. Remove the orange pieces. Serve the lamb with rice or couscous. Serves 2.

Chicken in Oatmeal

My grandmother cooked fish this way. She won't mind if you do.

¹/₂ cup/125 ml oats
  (the smaller the better)
¹/₂ tsp/2.5 ml dried thyme
¹/₂ tsp/2.5 ml dried tarragon
salt and pepper

2 boneless, skinless chicken
  breasts, cut into strips
1 egg, beaten
2 Tbsp/30 ml oil

Mix the oats, thyme, tarragon, salt and pepper together in a flat dish. Dip the chicken strips into the egg and then into the oat mixture. Heat the oil over high heat in a frypan. Add the chicken and reduce the heat to medium. Fry in the oil until lightly browned on both sides and cooked through, about 4 minutes each side. Serves 2.

Oatmeal Blueberry Pancakes

How to be popular with kids.

¹/₂ cup/125 ml
  quick-cooking oats
2 cups/500 ml buttermilk
2 eggs
1¹/₂ cups/375 ml flour
a pinch of salt
1 tsp/5 ml baking soda

1 Tbsp/15 ml sugar
¹/₂ tsp/2.5 ml cinnamon
a pinch of nutmeg
³/₄ cup/185 ml blueberries
2 Tbsp/30 ml oil
maple syrup
1 orange, sliced

Put the oats and buttermilk into a bowl and let them soak together for a few minutes, then beat in the eggs. Add the flour, salt, baking soda, sugar, cinnamon and nutmeg. Stir in the blueberries. Heat the oil in a frypan over medium heat and pour spoonfuls of the batter into the pan. Cook until bubbles form on the top, flip over and cook the other side until lightly browned. Serve with maple syrup and slices of orange. Serves 4 kids or 6 adults.

Oranges and Tequila

Dessert in a flash...

2 oranges, peeled and sliced $1/4$ cup/60 ml tequila
2 Tbsp/30 ml sugar

Lay the orange slices in a bowl and sprinkle the sugar over top. Pour the tequila over the slices and let them sit for an hour or so. Serves 2.

Spinach Salad with Feta and Oranges

1 bunch fresh spinach, washed $1/4$ cup/60 ml olive oil
   and drained, stems cut off   3 Tbsp/45 ml wine vinegar
2 oranges, peeled and chopped   1 tsp/5 ml balsamic vinegar
$1/2$ cup/125 ml feta cheese,   salt and pepper
   crumbled

Toss all of the ingredients together and serve immediately. Serves 4 as a side dish, or 2 with a good loaf of bread.

Moroccan Orange Salad with Cinnamon

4 oranges, peeled and sliced $1/2$ cup/125 ml walnuts,
1 Tbsp/15 ml sugar   toasted and chopped
$1/2$ tsp/2.5 ml cinnamon   a sprig of fresh basil, chopped

Toss all of the ingredients together and serve. Serves 4.

Toasted Oats and Black Bean Soup

Fifteen minutes...a real knife and fork soup.

1/2 cup/125 ml oats
1 tsp/5 ml cumin
1/2 tsp/2.5 ml chili powder
1 Tbsp/15 ml oil
1 onion, chopped
1 stalk celery, chopped
1 clove garlic, chopped
2 chilis

4 tomatoes, chopped
3-4 cups/750 ml - 1 litre stock
   or water
1-14 oz/398 ml tin black beans,
   drained and rinsed
a handful of cilantro, chopped
juice of 1 lime

*In a dry frypan, toast the oats, cumin and chili powder until the oats are lightly browned.
Heat the oil in a saucepan over high heat and cook the onion, celery, garlic and chili
peppers for 2 to 3 minutes, while stirring. Add the tomatoes, oat mixture and stock.
Bring to a boil, add the black beans, lower the heat and let simmer for 5 to 10 minutes.
Serve with a sprinkling of cilantro and a squeeze of lime juice. Serves 4.*

PEANUT BUTTER, PRUNES AND POETRY

Twice a year I go to France. Most of the time I spend just outside Toulouse. Toulouse is the gourmet's heaven, the Mecca to which all serious eaters must make a pilgrimage at least once in their lifetime. Almost everything in Toulouse is related to food or music—even the postcards in the tourist shops are about food. Vancouver may have pictures of the mountains and San Francisco the Golden Gate Bridge, but Toulouse has sausages on its cards. And ducks, and *foie gras*, and lots of close-ups of people with cloth napkins round their necks, shovelling *cassoulet* and *magret de canard* into their faces. Toulouse and good food are inseparable.

But, every time I go there I get the same request: "Bring peanut butter." It started off small (I thought it was a joke), and I took a small jar. Last time I took a five gallon pail, and my friends were swamped; the rumour was around, *"peanut butter"*, and all of their sophisticated French friends were bringing their little containers over, and dropping off, in return, all manner of expensive exotics. For some reason, peanut butter isn't available in France.

All kids, of course, like peanut butter. Not just the taste, but the texture, the sticky, *sucky* smoothness of it, the lovely way it gets between the teeth and stays there, the spare bits that stick to the roof of your mouth, the *squishiness* of it. Peanut butter isn't just food; it's a sensory experience, and adults, once they stop identifying it with Grade One lunch boxes, can easily get hooked on it.

I use peanut butter for a lot of cooking. Simplest of all, spread a little on the next hamburger patty you grill. Cook one side, flip over, and spread the peanut butter on the cooked side, so it will get warm without sticking to the grill. If you're broiling in the oven (or even in the toaster oven) the peanut butter will caramelize a bit and get bubbly on top. That's basic North American. Now let's get international. Almost everybody who has tried Greek or Middle Eastern food has eaten *hummus*, a dip made of *tahini*, which is basically ground sesame seeds, or even more simply, sesame seed butter.

But sesame seeds, or *tahini*, are very expensive. Peanut butter isn't, so next time you have a party, try this. Mix the juice of a lemon and two cloves of garlic, chopped fine, into two tablespoons (30 ml) of peanut butter. As you stir it (a fork works best) the peanut butter will get stiffer and thicker, but keep stirring. Now stir in plain yoghurt, a spoonful at a time, until it's all a nice creamy, dip-like consistency, just thick enough to stick to raw vegetables, but not thin enough to run down the front of your shirt. Sprinkle it with a little paprika, or ground red pepper. Serve it with a bowl of raw vegetables, or a crusty loaf torn into bits. And, look smug, because very few people will realize what it is, and they'll all want the recipe.

Kids seem to like this dip (you can put a little pot of it in a lunch box) and, just like *tahini*, it is remarkably good with fish, or chicken, or, thinned out a bit more with a little extra yoghurt, on cooked vegetables like broccoli or green beans.

That's Greece taken care of. Now Africa, where peanuts (called groundnuts, because they don't grow on trees, but in the soil like potatoes) are an important part of the diet. Vegetables, meat, fish—they can all be cooked with peanuts, and even more simply, they can all be cooked with peanut butter.

This recipe for chicken (call it African Chicken if you like) is a very easy, very quick, very different one-pot supper which you can have on the table 30 minutes after starting.

Toss enough cut-up chicken for four in one teaspoon (five ml) of turmeric, one teaspoon (five ml) of salt and one teaspoon (five ml) of curry powder. Fry it quickly in two tablespoons (30 ml) of oil (medium to high heat) with an inch (2.5 cm) or so of grated ginger-root, until the outsides are cooked. Add two cloves of chopped garlic, and a large onion cut into chunks. Cook another two minutes. Stir in three tablespoons (45 ml) of peanut butter, two large chopped-up tomatoes (or a half-can of tomatoes), one teaspoon (five ml) of ground black pepper, and a half-cup (125 ml) of water.

Bring to a boil, stirring well, and cook five minutes. Then add whatever cut-up vegetables you have on hand (celery, turnip, sweet potato, ordinary potato, carrot, mushrooms, leeks—but not *all* of them, just some). Stir well, and cook, covered, over low heat for 20 minutes. Stir and check occasionally; if it gets too dry or starts to stick to the pan, stir in half-a-cup (125 ml) of water. Serve it with rice, and if you want to be *really* fancy, sprinkle it with grated coconut and garnish with chopped parsley and thin slices of lemon. This will be elegant enough for a small dinner party.

If you want a change, then substitute pork chops for chicken, and sprinkle the finished dish with lots of finely chopped parsley. If you want to make it Malaysian style, then do exactly the same thing as above, but add a half-teaspoon (2.5 ml ml) of red cayenne pepper with the turmeric and salt, and squeeze a lime all over it just before serving. Peanut butter is very versatile.

Now, soup. There are fancy consommes in fancy restaurants, and there are cold soups and fruit soups and all manner of designer soups, but *soup*, to most people, is something warm and nourishing and chunky; it's comfort on a cold day, almost as good as a wood fire.

Unfortunately, it's also become one of those things that seems easier not to do. A little too much work, a vaguely remembered recipe, and the vague fear that it might not be *right*. So we open cans. But 30 minutes spent making a soup (and furnishing the kitchen with the rich warm smells of slow cooking), will make a family out of comparative strangers. Big bowls of a big, rich chunky soup, some good bread and then seconds. That's a memory that will last all your life; much longer than a Polaroid.

Soup with peanut butter may sound strange at first, but if you read the gourmet magazines you'll find all manner of recipes which tell you to spend all day searching out exactly the right size of peanuts, then roasting them, skinning them, grinding them and finally, two hours later finishing up with "the paste", which is then incorporated into a *soupe aux cacaouettes*.

You and me, we go to the store and buy a jar of peanut butter...

You also buy a big yam, a big onion, and some celery. Chop the onion, and cook it over medium heat in two tablespoons (30 ml) of oil or four tablespoons (60 ml) of butter for two minutes. Peel and slice the yam, chop four stalks of celery and add them to the onions and cook for five minutes. Sprinkle with a teaspoon (five ml) of curry powder and a teaspoon (five ml) of ground black pepper. Add eight cups (two litres) of water (or chicken stock), a bay leaf and a teaspoon (five ml) of dried thyme. Bring to a boil, and simmer slowly for 20 minutes. Stir in four tablespoons (60 ml) of peanut butter, add the juice of a lemon and then salt to taste.

You have two choices: first, to just *eat* it, chunky and hot, or to purée it in a blender or food processor. The puréed soup can be chilled, and kept for a couple of days, then eaten cold (or warmed in the microwave). It can be poured into bowls, with a spoonful of yoghurt in the centre, and sprinkled with either chopped parsley or coarse-chopped roasted peanuts (or both).

And, now, of course, you can see why my friends in France *covet* the stuff so much!

Hummus on the Cheap

Tahini is expensive, so I use peanut butter. The peanut butter smooths this out a bit, and gives it a richer flavour.

1-14 oz/398 ml tin chickpeas, drained and rinsed	4 Tbsp/60 ml peanut butter
	juice of 1 lemon
3 cloves garlic	6 Tbsp/90 ml yoghurt

Combine all of the ingredients in a food processor and whiz until smooth. For a thinner hummus, dilute with a little warm water, more lemon juice or more yoghurt, if necessary. Makes about 2 cups/500 ml.

JB's Peanut Sauce

This will keep in the fridge for a month, but will thicken until you warm it up again.

1-14 oz/398 ml tin coconut milk	juice of 1 lemon
	1/3 cup/85 ml soy sauce
1/3 cup/85 ml peanut butter	1/3 cup/85 ml water
3 cloves garlic	2 Tbsp/30 ml brown sugar
2 red chilis	2 Tbsp/30 ml sesame oil

Combine all of the ingredients in a food processor and whiz until creamy. Serve with rice or noodles or vegetables or barbecued meat or fish or just about anything. Makes about 3 cups/750 ml.

Tan Tan Noodles

1 cup/250 ml JB's peanut sauce
  (previous recipe)
1 cup/250 ml water or stock
3 cups/750 ml cooked noodles
cilantro, chopped

a handful of roasted peanuts,
  chopped
chili flakes
3 green onions, sliced thin

Combine the peanut sauce and stock together in a saucepan and heat until just boiling. Add the noodles, heat through and serve, sprinkled with chopped cilantro, peanuts, hot chili flakes and green onions. Serves 2.

Parsley Salsa Verde

Serve this over salads or sliced tomatoes, steamed potatoes, fish or chicken.

a handful of parsley
a handful of cilantro
1 green onion
juice of half-a-lemon

3 Tbsp/45 ml olive oil
3 Tbsp/45 ml cream
  or sour cream
salt and pepper

*Combine all ingredients in a food processor and blend until smooth.
Makes about 1 1/2 cups/375 ml.*

Skordalia

4 cloves garlic
salt and pepper
2 cups/500 ml mashed potatoes
1 slice white bread, no crust and crumbled

chopped parsley
1/3 cup/85 ml olive oil
juice of half-a-lemon

Mash the garlic, salt and pepper together and mix in with the potatoes. Add the bread and parsley, mix well and slowly beat in the oil. Squeeze the lemon juice over top and serve with pita bread or crackers. Makes about 2 cups/500 ml.

Turkish Parsley Soup

A cold soup or dip, the Turks call it "Tarator".

1 cucumber, chopped
3 cloves garlic, chopped
1/2 cup/125 ml walnuts
a handful of parsley

2 Tbsp/30 ml olive oil
1 cup/250 ml yoghurt
salt and pepper
1 thick slice french bread

Combine all ingredients in a food processor and blend until smooth. If a thinner consistency is desired, throw some ice cubes into the processor and whiz again. Serve cold. If you want to serve this as a dip, you'll need to add another slice of bread to the processor and whiz to thicken it up. Serve with more baguette. Serves 2.

Catalan Stewed Chicken

A 30 minute one-pot wonder.

2 Tbsp/30 ml oil
8 boneless, skinless
   chicken thighs, cut into
   bite-size pieces
1 onion, thinly sliced
1 clove garlic, chopped
2 tomatoes, chopped

1 cup/250 ml prunes
2 red peppers, chopped
1 bay leaf
2 Tbsp/30 ml parsley, chopped
1 tsp/5 ml thyme
1/4 cup/60 ml white wine
salt and pepper

Heat the oil in a frypan over high heat. Add the chicken and cook 2 to 3 minutes, stirring so it all gets browned. Add the onions and garlic and cook 3 to 4 minutes, until softened. Add the tomatoes, prunes, peppers, herbs and wine. Cover and let simmer for 30 minutes, or until the chicken is tender. Season and serve. Serves 4.

Leek and Potato Soup

The best of soups.

1 Tbsp/15 ml butter
2 leeks, finely chopped
1 large potato, peeled
   and grated
salt and pepper

1 1/2 cups/375 ml apple juice
   or water
1/3 cup/85 ml cream or yoghurt
2 Tbsp/30 ml chives, chopped

Melt the butter in a saucepan over medium heat and cook the leeks for 2 to 3 minutes, until softened. Add the potato and cook 2 more minutes. Season and pour in the apple juice. Cover and simmer for 7 to 8 minutes, or until the vegetables are tender. Blend in the food processor until smooth, and then stir in the cream. Serve hot or cold, garnished with chives. Serves 2.

Spicy Potato Pancakes

2 Tbsp/30 ml oil
2-3 potatoes, peeled,
   grated and squeezed dry
1 onion, grated
a bunch of fresh chives,
   chopped

1/2 cup/125 ml flour
2 eggs
1/2 tsp/2.5 ml turmeric
a pinch of cayenne
salt and pepper
1 tsp/5 ml cumin seeds

Heat the oil in a frypan over medium heat. Mix the potatoes, onion, chives, flour, eggs, turmeric and cayenne together to form a thick mixture. Season. Add the cumin seeds to the pan and cook for 30 seconds, then add some of the potato mixture to the pan, flattening with a spatula into round cakes. Cook 3 to 4 minutes, until golden. Flip and cook 2 minutes more. Serves 2.

QUAILS AND SOME QUAINT CHICKEN

A good roast chicken, brown and shiny on a plate, is not only a lovely thing to look at, but it is also one of the few things that the average cook, at home (and surrounded by the symphony of disasters and troubles that just being at home carries with it), can put on the table looking *even* better than the glossy magazine pictures.

Almost any chicken dish looks good. Baked, boiled, fried, steamed, poached, stewed or barbecued, there's very little you can do to a chicken to make it look like anything but a nice piece of chicken. You can cook it with bread-crumbs, with nuts, fruit, even peanut butter or marmalade and it still finishes up glamorous.

Most kids like chicken, even those who think that a can of spaghetti is the food of the gods, and the only religion chicken offends is vegetarian. It pleases almost everybody —there's white meat, dark meat, some pieces with a bone and some without. Dragged out of a dark corner of the freezer one Saturday night when company comes uninvited, and looks as if it won't leave before supper, almost any old bit of chicken lends itself to immediate improvisation. A few beans, a can of tomatoes, maybe some pasta—there's supper, and if you're bright enough to give it a fancy name, ("*Pollo Venezio*—my great-great-grandma was Italian…"), people will invariably like it, and ask you for the recipe.

But, despite this versatility, chicken still brings out the conservative in our kitchens. A US study which showed that most families had a maximum repertoire of 10 recipes (including such things as packaged hotcakes,

lasagna and muffin mix) also showed that *fried* chicken was one invariable constant. There's nothing wrong with that—dinner in a hurry, cooked on top of the stove, but there *are* alternatives to Shake n' Bake. No matter how much you like *The Sound of Music*, you don't watch it every night—you flip channels occasionally, and find something different.

Chicken's greatest virtue is its ability to absorb and amplify other flavors, so that each dish becomes something different. It also takes on different textures when it's combined with other ingredients. Chicken is also a wonderful thing to experiment with, to learn to cook with, because short of burning it you just can't go wrong. No matter what you do, *somebody* at the table is bound to say: "I really *like* chicken!"

The Chinese have a method of marinating chicken with cornstarch which produces a wonderfully smooth texture. They call it Velvet Chicken. It's very easy, very quick and fancy enough to serve the most critical of your friends. Breasts are best for the first time you do this one, because they slice easily, but once you know the technique, then thighs are a much better buy. You will need a sharp knife to take the bone out of the thighs, which is a lot easier than it sounds. Once they're out, you can make a nice little soup with them for next day's supper.

De-bone and skin two chicken breasts. Slice them crosswise about as thick as a pencil, and mix them well with one teaspoon (five ml) of cornstarch, one teaspoon (five ml) of vegetable oil, one half-teaspoon (2.5 ml) of salt and one half-teaspoon (2.5 ml) of ground pepper. Now mix 18 or 20 small fresh mushrooms (or four or five larger ones, quartered) with two teaspoons (10 ml) of cornstarch, one half-teaspoon (2.5 ml) of salt and one teaspoon (five ml) of ground pepper. Pour two thirds of a cup (170 ml) of very hot water over them (I take it straight from the tap). That's all the preparation.

Chop a piece of fresh ginger (about as big as your big toe), and fry it over medium-high heat in one tablespoon (15 ml) of vegetable oil, while you finely chop a clove of garlic. Add the garlic, stir it around for half-a-minute, turn the heat to high, and add the chicken, stirring it around quite vigorously for a minute. Add the mushrooms, liquid and all, stir well, and cook until the chicken is white and translucent (a maximum of five minutes). That's it, Velvet Chicken, and you serve it with rice.

You can pretty it up with chopped parsley, or chopped spring onion tops, or chopped chives; you can eat it with asparagus, or a salad. You can make the rice a rich golden colour by stirring turmeric into the cooking water; you can add more pepper if you like it spicier. You can sprinkle it with lemon juice, you can add a glass of sherry to the mushroom and cornstarch mixture if you have to impress somebody. And, if you want to go in for overkill, you look modest and tell them it's called *Mor Gwoo Gai Pien*. It's all dead easy—the only spice you need is pepper—and the real joy comes from the texture. Whatever you do, don't *overcook* it.

Now, let's move on to flavour, an Italian dish called *Piccata di Pollo*. Four minutes preparation, three minutes cooking, this is a real quickie, but it's also a dish that very fancy restaurants serve with pride and a hefty bill.

Once again, a chicken breast, de-boned and skinned. Sprinkle it lightly with flour, and put it between two sheets of waxpaper, or slide it carefully into a plastic bag. Pound it lightly with the side of a bottle (an oil bottle, a wine bottle, even a beer bottle—just pound it lightly, but firmly, all over, and it will spread to almost double its original size).

Now comes the fun part. You'll need some white wine (or some cider or some apple juice), some pepper, some salt and some butter. You'll need to have *everything* else for dinner ready—the flowers, the salad, the bread, the wine, a little chopped parsley and even somebody poised to say grace, because this is a quick one: it's ready almost before you can say "Wash your hands, please." It's also nice to have people standing around saying things like, "How *do* you do it?" and, "You're *so* quick…"

Ready? Heat a frypan big enough to cook one or two of the pieces of chicken. Add a lump of butter (about as big as your thumb), and as soon as it melts, put in the chicken. Cook it until the edges go white (about one minute) and *immediately* turn it over. Sprinkle with pepper and salt, cook for another minute, then slide it on to a plate. Add three tablespoons (45 ml) of wine or apple juice and the juice of half-a-lemon to the pan, boil it furiously for half-a-minute and pour over the chicken. Sprinkle with chopped parsley and serve immediately. This is not a dish you can do for 20 people—keep it for friends and family—your reputation will spread by word of mouth.

But if you *do* want a dinner for 20, there's nothing easier than *Chicken Cacciatore*, a dish which has managed to get itself seriously complicated since its first humble beginnings. In the days when hunters didn't have four-wheel drives to get them in and out of the woods before dark, they would frequently spend days tramping around, sometimes with their meat getting a *little* ripe. *Cacciatore* (hunter) style was a necessity, and the prime ingredient was vinegar, which counteracted the funky flavour of the meat. Sometimes, the vinegar wasn't even real vinegar, it was just wine going sour in an old-style leather bottle, but the effect was the same. And, everything else needed for cooking the meat was easily carried in the hunter's jacket pocket.

You need enough chicken for four. If you're buying cut-up chicken, this is the time to get thighs—more flavour, less money. Heat a frypan over medium heat for a couple of minutes, add three tablespoons (45 ml) of oil (vegetable, but preferably olive, for more flavour) and fry the chicken until it's golden all over. If the heat is too high the skin will shrink, so be patient, and turn it regularly. After five minutes of frying add pepper and salt, one half-teaspoon (2.5 ml) of dried rosemary and three cloves of garlic (unpeeled and unchopped). Five minutes later, add a quarter-cup (60 ml) of vinegar (which will bubble and spit a bit) and scrape off the bottom of the pan anything which may have stuck to it. Cover the pan, turn the heat down to simmer, and let it cook for 15 to 20 minutes. Remove the chicken and place on a warm serving plate. Now, turn up the heat and boil the sauce down until it's thick. If the sauce is already boiled down, then add one-quarter cup (60 ml) of water (or wine) and boil it down again. That's the sauce; pour it over the chicken and eat it with bread, boiled potatoes, or pasta.

And, the next time you're cooking chicken for the family, try adding just two tablespoons (30 ml) of vinegar for the last five minutes of cooking. You'll be surprised (I seem to say that to you regularly) but it won't be bitter at all; it'll have a nutty, almost caramel flavour once it's cooked.

Finally, the *definitive* roast chicken. Preheat the oven to 400F (190C). Rub a three or four pound (1.5 or 2 kg) chicken lightly with salt, lightly crush some rosemary with two or three cloves of garlic, mix it in with the juice of a lemon and pour everything into the back end of the chicken. Put the chicken into the hot oven for 15 minutes. Turn the heat down to 375F (190C) and cook for another 15 minutes. Reduce the heat to 350F (177C) and cook for another 30 to 45 minutes (until the leg wiggles easily in its socket). Remove from the oven and let it sit for 10 minutes, while you cook vegetables or make a salad, then sprinkle it with more lemon juice just before carving. Keep the carcass for soup. If you haven't got rosemary, then use thyme, or oregano, or tarragon.

All a chicken ever really needs is one fresh herb.

Roast Chicken with Lemons

2 Tbsp/30 ml flour
1 tsp/5 ml salt
$1/2$ tsp/2.5 ml pepper
6 chicken thighs
1 Tbsp/15 ml olive oil

zest and juice of lemon
2 cloves garlic, 1 chopped,
  1 halved
1 cup/250 ml seedless
  grapes

Preheat the oven to 375F (190C). Place flour, salt, pepper and chicken thighs in a plastic bag and shake until thighs are coated with flour. Heat the oil in a frypan over medium heat. Add the chicken and cook 2 minutes each side, until browned. Sprinkle with lemon juice, zest and chopped garlic. Grease an oven-proof dish and rub the dish with the 2 halves of garlic. Place the chicken in the dish, scatter the grapes over top and bake for 25 minutes, until chicken is cooked. Serves 4.

Chicken and Peanuts

The first Chinese food I ever ate...very easy.

1 tsp/5 ml cornstarch
2 Tbsp/30 ml soy sauce
2 Tbsp/30 ml whiskey
a pinch of cayenne pepper
$1/2$ tsp/2.5 ml salt
2 Tbsp/30 ml oil

2 skinless, boneless chicken
  breasts, cut into bite-size pieces
1 clove garlic, chopped
1 onion, chopped coarse
$1/4$ cup/60 ml water
1 cup/250 ml roasted peanuts

Mix the cornstarch, soy sauce, whiskey, cayenne pepper and salt together in a bowl to make a marinade. Add the chicken, toss and let it sit for a few minutes. Heat the oil in a frypan over medium heat. Add the chicken (hang on to the marinade) and cook for 1 minute, toss and add the garlic and onion. Cook 3 to 4 minutes, add the marinade and water and stir. Cook 3 to 4 more minutes, add the peanuts and mix together. Serves 2.

Cornish Game Hens and Raspberries

2 Cornish game hens,
  spatchcocked
3 Tbsp/45 ml olive oil
1 pkg frozen raspberries,
  thawed and drained
$^1/_2$ cup/125 ml apple juice
zest of 1 lemon

salt and pepper
1 Tbsp/15 ml butter
a handful of parsley, chopped
2 Tbsp/30 ml raspberry
  or balsamic vinegar
2 green onions, chopped

Heat the oil in a large frypan over high heat and add the hens. Brown both sides, then add the raspberries, apple juice and lemon zest and cook for 8 to 10 minutes. Sprinkle with salt and pepper and stir in the butter and chopped parsley. Just before serving, stir in the vinegar and sprinkle with chopped green onions. Serves 2.

Spatchcocked Quail and Grapes

'Spatchcocked' means that the backbone of the quail is cut out with a pair of scissors and the quail flattened. Use a pair of kitchen scissors to do the job. You can do the same thing with game hens, but they will take twice as long to cook.

3 Tbsp/45 ml olive oil
4 quails, spatchcocked
2 egg whites
4 Tbsp/60 ml cornmeal
1 Tbsp/15 ml butter

$^1/_2$ cup/125 ml almonds
2 cloves garlic, chopped
$^1/_2$ cup/125 ml seedless grapes
$^1/_2$ cup/125 ml cilantro
  or parsley, chopped

Heat the oil in a large frypan over high heat. Dip the quails in egg white and then cornmeal. Place them in the frypan and cook until brown on both sides (about 5 minutes each side). Remove them from the frypan and set them aside. Reduce the heat to medium-low and add the butter, almonds, garlic and grapes to the same frypan. Cook for 2 to 3 minutes and then stir in the chopped cilantro. Pour over the quails and serve immediately. Serves 4.

Chicken and Cucumbers

Very refreshing.

2 Tbsp/30 ml butter
2 boneless, skinless chicken
  breasts, cut into bite-size pieces
2 green onions, chopped
1/2 cucumber, peeled
  and chopped

1 tsp/5 ml fresh mint, chopped
1 Tbsp/15 ml parsley, chopped
1/2 cup/125 ml white wine
  or apple juice
2 Tbsp/30 ml yoghurt
salt and pepper

Melt the butter in a frypan over medium heat. Add the chicken and cook for 2 minutes, until browned all over. Add the green onions, cucumber, mint and parsley. Cook for 1 minute, then add the white wine. Cook for 5 minutes, until the liquid is almost gone. Stir in the yoghurt, season and serve over hot pasta or rice. Serves 2.

Satay

For the barbecue or oven, but I've even done this in a toaster oven.

1/2 lb/227 g skinless, boneless
  chicken, pork or beef,
  cut into bite-size pieces
8 bamboo skewers, soaked in
  water for 1/2 hour,
  or 8 small metal skewers
juice of half-a-lemon
1 Tbsp/15 ml oil

1 clove garlic, chopped fine
1 Tbsp/15 ml peanut butter
1 tsp/5 ml tomato paste
1 chili, chopped fine or
  1/2 tsp/2.5 ml dried chili flakes
3 Tbsp/45 ml water
1 tsp/5 ml soy sauce

Preheat the broiler. Place three or four pieces of meat on each skewer and sprinkle with lemon juice. Heat the remaining ingredients in a small pan over medium heat. Cook for a few minutes, stirring until smooth. Set aside. Cook the meat under the broiler for 3 minutes on each side, or until the meat is done. Serve as an appetizer with the sauce, hot or cold.

RICE, RISOTTO AND REMAINDERS

Rice, in my youth, was essential to Sunday. Rice pudding, stodgy as an ageing bath sponge, skinned and blistered on top like a bad sunburn, and served with Bird's Custard, a vivid yellow sludge the consistency of latex paint—I didn't like rice pudding and I knew of no other way to eat it.

A nice woman in Sienna took me to her house, her kitchen, and her bosom. We ate a lot of *risotto*; rice gently and slowly cooked in a mixture of white wine and chicken stock, and because there is no way you can make a risotto in less than 20 minutes (or more than 25) we invented a number of ways to entertain ourselves for slightly less than half-an-hour. Since then, I have been quite sure that the making of a good risotto is an almost infallible criterion for choosing a partner, short or long term. A gentle hand, a lightness of touch, a sense of proportion and above all, knowing when to stop. All of these are as essential to the art of risotto as they are to what some call the art of love. But risotto is easier to learn and teaches patience. It also teaches texture, which I never know for sure is the feel of taste or the taste of feel.

Rice is *not* the pure stodge found in English boarding schools. I remember discovering *congee*, which is really a kind of rice soup, made by cooking rice *very* slowly in a lot of water (eight cups of water to one cup of rice). I had a stomach tired of travelling and refusing to cooperate the way stomachs are supposed to. Every country has grandmas and the one who found me in Thailand brought me congee, with shredded ginger cooked in it; soft, gentle and soothing as a Japanese massage. Next morning my stomach was happy to continue living. It takes three hours to make at home—easy if you can sit by a small stove and occasionally stir—but Chinese restaurants will always, for very little money, sell you a bowl.

Now leftovers. Always cook twice as much rice as you plan on eating, and then keep it covered in the refrigerator. Refried, with a little oil, a little chopped onion, almost *anything* green chopped up and some bits of leftover meat. You have a meal ready in 10 minutes—15, if you want to put fancy things in it.

Cold rice mixed with a beaten egg for breakfast pancakes; cold rice with a simple vinaigrette and some chopped green onions for a salad; cold rice mixed with a few raisins and a little cream for dessert. There's no end to what you can do with rice when you add a few simple ingredients.

And then, of course, there's *sake*, a wine made from rice; the most comforting of all drinks on a winter's day.

Quick Rice Pudding

¼ cup/60 ml light cream	1 tsp/5 ml brown sugar
¼ tsp/1 ml cinnamon	2 Tbsp/30 ml raisins
a pinch of allspice	1 cup/250 ml cooked rice

Heat the cream, spices, sugar and raisins in a small saucepan over medium heat, but do not let it boil. Stir into the rice and serve. Serves 1.

Herbed Risotto

Much more than just rice.

2 Tbsp/30 ml olive oil
1/2 an onion, finely chopped
1 clove garlic, chopped
1 tsp/5 ml thyme
1/2 tsp/2.5 ml sage
1 tsp/5 ml rosemary
2 Tbsp/30 ml parsley, chopped
2 Tbsp/30 ml mint, chopped

1 cup/250 ml short grain
   (arborio) rice
1/2 cup/125 ml white wine or,
   in a pinch, apple juice
3 cups/750 ml stock or water
2 Tbsp/30 ml parmesan
salt and pepper

Heat the oil in a large frypan over high heat, and add the onion and garlic. Cook for 2 to 3 minutes, or until the onion is softened. Stir in the herbs and rice, and cook for 2 minutes, until the rice is translucent. Reduce the heat to medium, add the wine and stir until it has almost all evaporated. Stir in half-a-cup of stock (125 ml). Keep stirring it until the liquid is all gone, then add another half-cup of stock. Repeat until you've used it all up. When the rice feels thick, but cooked, stir in the parmesan, season and serve immediately. Serves 2.

Apple Rum Risotto

There aren't too many stove top desserts as good as this.

4 Tbsp/60 ml butter
1 apple, peeled, cored
   and chopped small
1 1/2 cups/375 ml short grain
   (arborio) rice

2 1/2 Tbsp/37.5 ml sugar
1 Tbsp/15 ml rum
1 Tbsp/15 ml vanilla
5 cups/1.25 litres apple juice

Melt the butter in a large skillet over medium heat. Add the apple and rice and cook for 2 minutes. Add the remaining ingredients, bring to a boil and reduce the heat. Let the rice simmer until the liquid has evaporated (stirring occasionally) about 20 minutes. Serve immediately. Serves 4.

Bachelor's Fried Rice

2 Tbsp/30 ml oil
2 onions, chopped fine
pepper
2 cloves garlic, chopped
4 mushrooms, sliced thin
1-7 oz/196 ml tin shrimp,
   drained and rinsed
2 Tbsp/30 ml turmeric

3 cups/750 ml cooked rice
1/2 cup/125 ml green peas
a handful of bean sprouts
2 Tbsp/30 ml water
1 egg, beaten
2 green onions, chopped,
   cut in 1 inch/2.5 cm lengths

Heat the oil in a large frypan over medium heat. Add the onion and lots of pepper and cook for 2 to 3 minutes. Add the garlic and mushrooms and cook a further 2 to 3 minutes. Add the remaining ingredients except for the egg and green onions. Stir until well-combined and cook for 5 minutes. Pour the egg over top and stir until it has cooked in the mixture, about 2 minutes. Serve immediately, with green onions sprinkled over top. Serves 2.

Caponata Rice Salad

With anything barbecued.

1/4 cup/60 ml olive oil
2 cloves garlic, chopped
1 onion, chopped
1 zucchini, chopped
zest and juice of 1 lemon
2 tomatoes, chopped
1/2 cup/125 ml pitted
   black olives, chopped

2 Tbsp/30 ml capers
1 tsp/5 ml salt
1/2 tsp/2.5 ml pepper
2 cups/500 ml cold cooked rice
a handful of parsley,
   chopped

Heat 2 tablespoons/30 ml of the oil in a frypan over high heat. Add the garlic, onion and zucchini and cook for 2 to 3 minutes. Remove from heat and add the lemon juice. Toss the remaining ingredients together, add the zucchini mixture, toss with rice, sprinkle with parsley and serve. Serves 2.

Rice Pancakes

1 Tbsp/15 ml butter
1/2 an onion, chopped fine
2 green onions, chopped fine
salt and pepper

1/2 tsp/2.5 ml thyme
2 cups/500 ml cooked rice
2 eggs
2 Tbsp/30 ml olive oil

Melt the butter in a frypan over medium heat. Add the onion and green onions and cook until softened. Season with salt, pepper and thyme. Remove from heat and stir in the rice. Let the mixture cool, stir in the eggs and then shape it into small patties. Heat the oil in a frypan over high heat and cook the pancakes 1 to 2 minutes on each side. Serves 2 as a side dish.

Nasi Goreng

Bright and cheerful, a good dish with a small case of beer.

2 Tbsp/30 ml oil
1 skinless, boneless
   chicken breast,
   cut into bite-size pieces,
   or diced ham
1 chili, chopped
1/2 tsp/2.5 ml curry powder
   or turmeric
1 onion, chopped
2 cloves garlic, chopped

1 inch/2.5 cm fresh ginger,
   grated
2 Tbsp/30 ml soy sauce
1 Tbsp/15 ml sugar
1-7 oz/196 g tin shrimp,
   drained and rinsed
4 cups/1 litre cooked rice
1 inch/2.5 cm cucumber,
   grated

Heat the oil in a saucepan over medium heat. Add the chicken or ham, chili and curry powder, and cook for 2 to 3 minutes, until the chicken changes colour. Add the onion, garlic and ginger and cook for 2 to 3 minutes. Stir in the soy sauce, sugar and shrimp. Cook for 1 minute, then stir in the rice and heat through. Serve immediately, with grated cucumber on top. Serves 4.

SIMPLY SOUPER

Soups are at their best when they just happen. Consommés need care; they need to be skimmed and degreased and clarified and looked after; *veloutes* need work and lots of expensive ingredients. But, soups, whether they be called *potages* or *touraines* or *matelote*, are dishes of love which arrive far more by accident than by design.

My most favoured soup comes right after Christmas or Thanksgiving. I give the turkey my best shot, with all the trimmings, the chestnut stuffing, the baked whole onions, the brussels sprouts cooked in butter with sliced almonds and the potatoes mashed with turnips and much too much pepper. And I'm happy to see it shining on a great big platter with all the smiling faces sitting around it.

But, when the party's over, the dishes done and the goodbyes all waved, the fact of the turkey still remains. It doesn't just sit in the fridge, it *occupies* it, and it looks as sad and passively demanding as a dog with no dinner. Until it goes away, (until you've actually eaten it), it continues with this ongoing daily reproach, leering at you every time you open the door, and sniggering when you've closed it.

Conscience won't let you throw it out, and it becomes part of the family. So, I make a soup, which completely disposes of the turkey, and I have another big party the next day; a *soup party* for a different lot of people, with big loaves of fresh rye bread, and if they ask, "What can I bring?", I tell them beer.

The soup is as simple as it is outrageous. Everything that was left on the table (except dessert, except whipped cream and mayonnaise) all goes into a pot: the salad (even Caesar salad), the dressing and *all* the vegetables; potatoes, brussels sprouts, mushrooms, carrots, parsnips, onions, pickles, cranberry sauce—everything goes in. Any large and easily removed meat on the turkey I pull off the carcass and store in a tidy container. What's left goes into the pot. It cuts up easily with shears, or you can break it down to size with your hands.

Cover everything with a hand's depth of water, bring it to the boil and let it simmer, covered, with the lid just tilted, for three or four hours. Strain it through a colander, let it cool (outside the back door or on the balcony). Skim off the fat on top.

What you now have is a wonderful and unpredictable soup. If there were anchovies in the salad (or apples), it won't taste the same as if there were oranges. Some dressings have rosemary and some have thyme; some people cook mushrooms with mint leaves, and some with tarragon. Each of these variations makes its *own* contribution to the soup, and each year that you make it, it will be different.

One hour before your guests come, heat up the strained soup, slice the bread and put the bowls in the oven to warm. Half-an-hour before they come, chop an onion or two, a tomato or three, and some celery if you have it. Cut up the turkey meat into bite-size pieces and add it all to the soup. Now comes the flavouring. I like grated fresh ginger root, but a teaspoon (five ml) of rosemary or thyme is fine. I add half-a-teaspoon (2.5 ml) of hot red pepper, a lot of black pepper, and I mix two teaspoons (10 ml) of cornstarch in a cup with a jigger of whiskey (apple juice works almost as well).

When everybody has arrived, you stir the cornstarch into the soup and let it simmer until it looks translucent. Now you add three or four tablespoons (60 ml) of vinegar, cook for two minutes and serve immediately. "Hot and sour soup", they will say, "My favourite, aren't you clever!" You just look modest and tell them that the secret is in *not* adding the vinegar until the last minute.

The basis of all good soups is stock, for which all fancy cookbooks have recipes. But most peasant families have the same recipe as we used for the turkey—they simmer leftovers on the stove all night, strain out the solids (which they feed to the chickens) and that's their stock. I buy chicken backs (and chicken feet), and sometimes, on wet and wintry Saturday afternoons, I fill a pot and let it simmer, with a few onions, some carrots and a bay leaf thrown in. I strain it, put it in storage containers, and freeze it. For the next month you have soup on demand—just fish out a container of stock, run it under the hot water tap and put it in a saucepan on low heat to melt.

For a quick vegetable soup, add chopped vegetables. A teaspoon (five ml) of oregano will make the vegetable soup into an Italian vegetable soup and a chopped tomato will move it into a minestrone; half-a-dozen garlic cloves will transform it into the sort of thing they make in the fall in the South of France, and a few slices of salami will turn it into a meal. (A slice of good bread simmered in with everything else will thicken and enrich it). Italians keep the rinds of their parmesan cheese, and simmer those in the pot, along with everything else, and if you do this, add a bunch of chopped basil, and you will suddenly have something the French call a *pistou*.

All it takes to make a good soup is a little patience and a little confidence in your ability to taste. The taste of stock is actually quite bland, but it does give the soup *body*. What ingredients you add will determine the final character. Most soups need salt, but you never add it until just before serving, because the process of cooking, and the evaporation will concentrate it.

In Southern France they grow a lot of oats to feed cattle. In winter, when food is scarce, they make a *potage a l'avoine*, which is simply a litre (four cups) of stock, four heaped tablespoons (60 ml) of oatmeal (porridge oats will do) and a lump of butter a bit bigger than a walnut. Just put the stock and oatmeal in a saucepan, and bring to the boil. Simmer, covered for 30 minutes, until it looks thick and rich. Add a little salt, and serve immediately, with a knob of butter swirled in. This is a good and simple soup, which can be made bigger by floating a poached egg in each plate, or by sprinkling it with chopped parsley, or by adding thin slices of spicy sausage. In its basic form, this soup has kept many a family healthy through a long mountain winter. And this is what a lot of "peasants" will be eating this year in France. Did you know that winter was invented so that we could all become peasants, and *enjoy* soup?

Turkeys came much, much later.

Sopa de Tortilla

Mexico in a bowl.

1 Tbsp/30 ml oil
1/2 an onion, chopped
1 jalapeño pepper, chopped
4 cloves garlic, chopped
2 tomatoes, chopped
4 cups/1 litre stock

a handful of cilantro,
  chopped
a handful of tortilla chips
a pinch of salt
grated cheddar
juice of 1 lime

Heat the oil in a frypan over high heat and cook the onion, jalapeño and garlic until softened. Combine in a food processor with the tomatoes, stock and cilantro. Blend until smooth and place the mixture in a saucepan. Bring to a boil. Put some tortilla chips in the bottom of a soup bowl and pour the soup over top. Season and sprinkle with grated cheese and serve with a squeeze of lime juice and extra cilantro. Serves 2.

Cream of Chickpea Soup

A real belly warmer.

2 Tbsp/30 ml oil
1 onion, chopped
3 cloves garlic, chopped
1 chili
1 carrot, chopped
a sprig of oregano or
  1 tsp/5 ml dried

1/2 tsp/2.5 ml cumin
4 cups/1 litre stock
1-19 oz/540 g tin chick peas,
  drained and rinsed
a bunch of parsley, chopped
1/2 cup/125 ml yoghurt
salt and pepper

Heat the oil in a pot over high heat. Add the onion, garlic, chili and carrot. Cook for 2 minutes, then add the remaining ingredients except the yoghurt. Bring to a boil, reduce heat and let simmer for 10 minutes. Pour the soup into a food processor and blend until smooth. Season and stir in the yoghurt. Sprinkle with more parsley and serve. Serves 4.

Chilled Cucumber Soup

2 cucumbers, chopped
zest and juice of 1 lime
$1/2$ tsp/2.5 ml salt
a handful of cilantro, chopped

$1/4$ cup/60 ml water
   or cold stock
yoghurt or sour cream
handful of shrimp (optional)

Place all ingredients into a food processor and whiz until smooth. Serve with a dollop of yoghurt or sour cream. Serves 4 as an appetizer.

Melon and Tomato Soup

3 tomatoes
1 cantaloupe, rind
   and seeds removed
zest and juice of 1 lime
$1/4$ cup/60 ml mint

half-a-cucumber
a pinch of salt
2 Tbsp/30 ml pepper
a pinch of cayenne
$1/2$ cup/125 ml yoghurt

Place all ingredients in a food processor and blend until smooth. Chill or serve at room temperature. Serves 4.

Lentil Soup with Orange

Canned lentils are quick, dried lentils will take 20 minutes longer.

2 Tbsp/30 ml oil
1 onion, chopped
1 clove garlic, chopped
1 tsp/5 ml ground cumin
2 tsp/10 ml ground coriander

zest and juice of 1 orange
3 cups/750 ml stock
1-19 oz/540 g tin lentils,
   drained and rinsed
salt and pepper

Heat the oil in a large pot over high heat. Add the onion, garlic and spices and cook for 2 to 3 minutes. Add the orange zest and juice, stir, and add the stock and lentils. Bring to a boil and cook 5 to 6 minutes, season and serve. Serves 2.

TURNING TRICKS FOR TWO WITH TOFU

Getting *too* intimate with food can be a problem, as anybody who has ever taken a high-chair baby to a restaurant rapidly finds out…

I have a good friend in the Comox Valley, on Vancouver Island, who is a single mother and a determined survivor, who buys a calf every spring and raises it on the pasture behind her house. Young calves are pretty, big-eyed and cuddly, and her children loved the first one, which they called Alfred.

In the fall, when Alfred disappeared and came back wrapped and labelled, "roasts", "steaks" and "stews", every dinner became a tearsome funeral, and the kids, for weeks, left Alfred (or anything which might once have been Alfred) sitting on the side of their plates, while they concentrated on potatoes and cabbage. Obviously, Alfred had never been a pig, but pork chops, sausages and bacon were also rejected, in favour of previously unpopular vegetables.

The next calf, equally big-eyed and cuddly, was christened even before it arrived. Not Alfred, not Boo-Boo nor Mitsy, but simply "D*inner*" and thus, it was introduced to the children. Since then, every calf they have raised has enjoyed the same name: "Here, Dinner, good boy…". There are no more illusions and no more heartbreaks.

Now, being vegetarian is perfectly understandable, but it used to be difficult, it wasn't much fun, and it always seemed to be a very expensive way of life.

The stores which sold vegetarian products not only charged an arm and a leg (or a leaf and a branch?) for it, but they seemed to share the old-fashioned idea that being vegetarian was somehow especially *virtuous*, and that virtue, to be properly appreciated, needed to be unpleasant. A sort of…medicine.

Their shelves were filled with "mock" stuff—mock duck and mock ham and soy "steaks". Something I remember as being particularly horrible was a "nut loaf", which looked like cold porridge, tasted like sawdust jello and claimed, on the label, to "appeal to children just as much as cake". Nobody seemed to think that a vegetarian diet could be a simple pleasure in its *own* right, and that it didn't have to pretend to be something else, or, even worse, always be doing you some good. (The first rule of eating is to enjoy it, and to remember the Greek benediction: "Food is good.").

It will be a long time before North America weans itself from a predominantly meat-filled diet, but we *are* learning to like something other than steak or hamburger. Restaurants, which until very recently, treated vegetarians like pet rabbits—and thought that providing extra large bowls of green salad was the answer—have now discovered that vegetables make more profit than meat; they're now putting all manner of unfamiliar, meatless items on their menus.

I am not a vegetarian—I can't keep my wheels turning without some animal protein, but I don't eat *much* meat. I think it was the Italians who taught me the special pleasures of vegetables. Italian restaurants in Italy serve vegetables as a separate course, not just dumped on the plate with the meat and potatoes. They present them carefully, as something for special enjoyment, and it's quite remarkable to watch even young children getting enthusiastic about artichokes, and chickpeas, or chicory—things which we have somehow taught our kids to be very suspicious of.

There's a lot to be said for eating sensible food, or food that's good for you, but the only way to encourage anybody to eat anything at *all* different is to make sure they enjoy it. That's how kids learn to eat, and that's how adults develop palates. Just stuffing spinach into reluctant mouths will get you nowhere, but put a little soy sauce on it, sprinkle it with sesame seeds and tell everybody it's a special Japanese dish…they'll eat it, and enjoy it.

The real art of successful vegetarian cooking is glamorizing otherwise very ordinary dishes. Take dried beans, simple white beans. Soak, and then cook them until they're tender and drain off any water left in the pot. Chop an onion, some garlic and a tomato, and stir them into the warm beans with salt, pepper, a good teaspoon (five ml) of oregano, a can of tuna and four tablespoons (60 ml) of olive oil. Sprinkle the whole thing with finely chopped parsley, and you have *Fagioli al Tonno*, to be eaten hot, warm or cold; as an appetizer or, with a slice of good bread, a green salad and a glass of wine, as a main course. It's not just beans any more.

It seems that the most essential ingredient of vegetarianism (at least my brand of vegetarianism, which, as I said before, springs from the Italians), is good olive oil, which is not only good for you (it actually dissolves cholesterol), but also tastes good and is much more digestible than butter.

The gourmet magazines will insist on extra virgin olive oil, which nine times out of 10 is nonsense. *Extra virgin* (supposedly the first pressing of ripe olives) has become little more than a name for the mass-marketers. The only *real* extra virgin oil is produced by a very small number of very small estates, and it's so expensive that it's often measured out right at the table with a teaspoon. Real Extra Virgin olive oil is much too expensive to cook with, and heat can easily destroy its delicate flavour. But a tablespoon or two added to a salad (or beans) will make a dramatic difference—you'll taste the rich freshness of good olives, and, like the Italians, you'll dip your bread in any oil left at the bottom of the dish. You may never want to eat butter again.

A lot of Italian household cooking is done with much less expensive oil—canola, safflower, sunflower or any vegetable oil. Grape seed oil is light and slightly nutty, with a distinctive flavour, and cold-pressed peanut oil, which is definitely *not* Italian, but is wonderful on salads. (It's a thick, occasionally cloudy oil which is also—because of its high smoke point—good for frying.)

So, let's look at salads—Italian style—which taste of the vegetable, the oil, and much *less* vinegar than we're used to. Fill half of a spice jar with oil, add the vinegar (which will stay separate from the oil and sink to the bottom of the jar so that you can easily measure it) until there is about three times as much oil as vinegar. Add a little salt, a little pepper, any herbs or spices that take your fancy, screw the lid on and shake well. This will emulsify the dressing. That's the basic, all purpose dressing. Now you can add an egg yolk, some mustard, or curry powder, soy sauce or garlic or chopped onion. Chopped anchovies are nice in a dressing, and sesame seeds—fried for a minute in a dry pan—go very well with soy sauce. If you want to replace the vinegar with orange or lemon or even grapefruit juice, you'll be surprised and delighted. All you need to start with is the little jar and a little imagination.

Warm (or wilted) salads don't have to be made of spinach and they don't need bacon bits. A handful of sliced fresh mushrooms warmed through in a frypan with any of these dressings will make a nice little supper on rice, or slices of fried bread (which the gourmets call *croutons*). A handful of nuts (walnuts, hazelnuts, even peanuts) tossed over medium heat for five minutes in a frypan, then mixed with two tablespoons (30 ml) of your dressing and poured over lettuce becomes an Italian salad from Sicily— the nuts crunchy, the dressing smooth and velvety and the lettuce crisp. All it needs is sliced fresh bread.

Seedless grapes warmed through in two or three tablespoons (30-45 ml) of dressing are a fine addition to an ordinary salad—so are sliced strawberries. Oranges, peeled and separated into segments make a very pleasant warm salad with almost any leaf vegetable. The nicest orange salad I know of is simply a couple of nice juicy oranges, sliced crosswise very thin (with the peel still on). Overlap the slices on a pretty plate, drizzle two tablespoons (30 ml) of your best oil over it, sprinkle generously with pepper and let it sit for half-an-hour.

Or hard-boiled eggs, halved, and laid cut-side down on a plate onto which you have poured a pool of lightly curry-flavoured dressing. Sprinkle with finely chopped parsley. Or steam asparagus (young green beans will also do) for seven minutes in a pan with three tablespoons (45 ml) of water and three tablespoons (45 ml) of dressing. Topped with two poached eggs; you'll be eating the way they do in Milan. A little jar, a little imagination, and not so much vinegar…

That's what I call vegetarian cooking!

Breakfast Tofu with Maple Syrup

Trust me... just TRY it!

1 Tbsp/15 ml oil	maple syrup
1 Tbsp/15 ml soy sauce	1 grapefruit, halved
1 pkg firm tofu, cut into finger-size strips	a pinch of cayenne

Heat the oil and soy sauce in a frypan over high heat. Add the tofu and cook until browned on both sides. Drizzle with maple syrup, squeeze the juice from the grapefruit over top, sprinkle with just a bit of cayenne and serve. Serves 2.

Sweet Potato and Tofu Curry

Carnivores like this too.

2 Tbsp/30 ml oil
1 tsp/5 ml cumin
1 onion, chopped
1 inch/2.5 cm fresh ginger,
  grated
1 Tbsp/15 ml curry powder
1 sweet potato, peeled and
  cut into chunks
$1/2$ cup/125 ml water
1 red pepper, chopped

1 pkg medium tofu,
  cut into chunks
$1/4$ head cauliflower,
  cut into small pieces
$1/2$ head broccoli,
  cut into small pieces
juice of half-a-lemon
salt and pepper
a handful of cilantro,
  chopped

Heat the oil in a saucepan or wok over high heat. Add the cumin, onion, ginger, curry powder and sweet potato and cook for 2 to 3 minutes. Add the water, cover and reduce the heat to medium-low. Cook for 20 minutes, then add the remaining ingredients. Cook, covered, for 5 more minutes and serve over rice. Serves 4.

Vietnamese Lettuce Wraps

2 Tbsp/30 ml oil
1 pkg firm tofu, crumbled
  or grated
$1/2$ a sweet pepper, chopped
2 green onions, chopped
1 tomato, chopped
1 carrot, grated

a sprig of basil, chopped,
  or 1 tsp/5 ml dried
1 tsp/5 ml cumin
a dash of soy sauce
a dash of sesame oil
1 head iceberg lettuce

Heat the regular oil in a large frypan or wok over high heat and add the tofu, sweet pepper, green onions, tomato, carrot, basil and cumin. Cook for 2 to 3 minutes and add the soy sauce and sesame oil. Toss well and remove from heat. Spoon some of the tofu mixture onto a lettuce leaf and roll it up. Serve with a bit of soy sauce on the side for dipping. Serves 4.

Tofu and Shrimp

2 Tbsp/30 ml oil

1 pkg firm tofu, cut into
   sugar cube-size chunks

2 inches/5 cm fresh ginger,
   grated

2 chilis

1/2 a red pepper, chopped

1/2 a green pepper, chopped

2 cups/500 ml uncooked shrimp

2 Tbsp/30 ml soy sauce

a handful of cilantro, chopped

a handful of bean sprouts

juice of 1 lime

1 Tbsp/15 ml sesame oil

2 green onions, chopped fine

Heat the oil in a wok or large frypan over high heat. Add the tofu and ginger and cook until they start to brown. Add the chilis, peppers and shrimp. Stir in the soy sauce and cook for 1 minute. Add the remaining ingredients, cook for 2 minutes, toss and serve when the shrimp have just turned pink. Serves 2.

Tofu and Red Onions in Pita

Chunky and very Greek, even though you can't find tofu in Greece.

1 Tbsp/15 ml oil

1 red onion, sliced thin

1 clove garlic, finely chopped

1/2 pkg medium tofu,
   cut into slices

1 Tbsp/15 ml soy sauce

a pinch of cayenne

juice of half-a-lemon

2 pita breads, cut in half

lettuce or spinach

2 Tbsp/30 ml yoghurt

1 avocado, peeled and sliced

Heat the oil in a frypan over high heat. Add the onion, garlic and tofu and cook until lightly browned. Stir in the soy sauce, cayenne and lemon juice. Open up the pita breads and line the insides with lettuce or spinach leaves. Pile the tofu mixture into the bottom and top with yoghurt and slices of avocado. Serves 2.

Tofuburgers

I was skeptical, but we worked at it.
Frying (instead of barbecuing) gives them a special richness.

1 pkg medium tofu,
  crumbled or grated
1 egg
1/2 cup/125 ml fresh
  breadcrumbs
1/2 cup/125 ml ground almonds
1/2 tsp/2.5 ml ground coriander
a sprig of fresh parsley, chopped
1 carrot, grated
1 Tbsp/15 ml mustard

a pinch of cayenne
2 cloves garlic, chopped
2 green onions, chopped
3 sprigs of basil, chopped
  or 1 tsp/5 ml dried
1/2 tsp/2.5 ml ground cumin
a splash of soy sauce
1 Tbsp/15 ml sesame oil
2 Tbsp/30 ml oil
yoghurt

Combine all of the ingredients except the regular oil to form a moist and sticky mixture
(if it's too moist, add more breadcrumbs). Form the mixture into hamburger-size patties.
Heat the oil in a frypan over high heat and add the patties. Lower the heat to medium
and cook for 4 to 5 minutes on each side, or until nicely browned and firm. Serve
on hamburger buns with a dollop of yoghurt on top. Makes 4 big burgers.

UNLIKELIES

"**M**arriage", said Oscar Wilde, "is the triumph of experiment over experience". And, while this may be true of the strange couplings that—in their *uncouplings*—make so much money for the divorce lawyers, it's a different story when it comes to the kitchen, and that lovely French culinary term, *"le marriage"*.

The one essential ingredient in any good kitchen (or any good relationship) is time; the time for things to come together. Instant food and junk food aren't part of the marriage process and they're no more satisfying than one night stands.

The main difference between a wonderful meal and a dull one is either time, or care, or both. Time doesn't have to be measured in hours—it's just the *right* time to let flavours either mingle or to keep them separate and distinct (like vinegar in hot and sour soup—if it goes in much before the last five minutes of cooking, it gets lost). And care? I think it has something to do with you becoming so involved in what you're doing that you find yourself salivating over the pot, licking your lips and sometimes (it happens to me with something as mundane as buttering toast) just quietly smiling.

Unusual couplings mean adventure. Fresh ground pepper on strawberries you may have tried, so go ahead and do the same thing with slices of very ripe melon. Close your eyes for a moment, and you'll have a full understanding of a summer spent in Persia.

You're now travelling on your own, not on a tour bus with everybody else.

The balsamic vinegar you got for Christmas looks *too* good and *too* expensive to experiment with. Where and how will you use it without being *brave*? Go back to those strawberries, the ones you so reluctantly put pepper on, and try just one drop of that wonderful, dark brown balsamic vinegar on each one. The next time; maybe a few shrimp, some slices of mango, a small dash of the balsamic vinegar and a very small sprinkling of curry powder. You're playing; you're painting; you're an artist and suddenly *everything* has a special flavour.

Ice cream made of avocado with coffee and lemon—just whiz a ripe avocado with the juice of a lemon, two tablespoons (30 ml) of honey or sugar and half-a-teaspoon (2.5 ml) of instant coffee, then fold in an equal amount of whipped cream.

Stir a teaspoon (five ml) of dried mint into your chili five minutes before serving. Make a pesto using cilantro instead of basil and use walnuts instead of pine nuts. Fry a handful of grapes and a little grated ginger with your chicken breast.

That's really what *fusion cooking* is about. And, you don't need to wear a tall white hat and you don't need a degree from a trendy cooking school. This kind of cooking is quite simply about *you* being unusual and having a good time doing it!

You never go looking for your own true love with a prescription in your hand. The same kind of thinking applies to food.

Watermelon Juice

Terrific on hot days.

4 cups/1 litre watermelon,
cut into small chunks
2 Tbsp/30 ml sugar

juice of 1 lime
a handful of ice cubes

Combine all of the ingredients in a blender and whiz until smooth.
Makes about 4 cups.

Layered Tortilla Pie

When us guys sit around.

2 Tbsp/30 ml oil
1 tsp/5 ml cumin
1 onion, chopped
2 tomatoes, chopped
2 chilis, chopped
1 green pepper, chopped
2 cloves garlic, chopped

1 pkg (6 or 8) 9-inch/22.5 cm
flour tortillas
1-14 oz/398 ml tin refried beans
1 tsp/5 ml cumin
1-14 oz/398 ml tin corn (kernels)
2 cups/500 ml grated cheese
a handful of cilantro, chopped

Preheat oven to 375F (190C). Heat the oil in a frypan over high heat and add the cumin, onion, tomatoes, chilis, green pepper and garlic. Cook for 5 to 6 minutes, until thickened. Place a tortilla in the bottom of a round 9-inch/22.5 cm casserole dish or springform pan. Top with a layer of the tomato mixture, a layer of beans and $1/2$ cup/125 ml of cheese. Top with another tortilla and repeat layering, adding a layer of corn and cilantro. Repeat layering until all the ingredients have been used up. Top with a tortilla and a sprinkling of grated cheese. Cover with foil and bake for 20 to 30 minutes. Remove from oven, let sit for 5 minutes, then slice into wedges and serve. Makes one big 9-inch/22.5 cm pie. Serves at least 4.

Italian Carrots and Grapes

When the new wine is ready for tasting, this dish often appears at the vineyard dinners.

2 Tbsp/30 ml oil
1 bunch or bag baby carrots,
   cleaned and left whole
1 cup/250 ml white wine or
   cider or apple juice

a large handful of seedless grapes
a sprig of fresh dill, chopped
salt and pepper
1 Tbsp/15 ml honey
a sprig of fresh mint, chopped

*Heat the oil in a saucepan over high heat. Add the carrots and wine and cook for
4 to 5 minutes. Add the grapes and dill and cook for 2 more minutes.
Season and serve drizzled with honey and with mint sprinkled on top. Serves 2.*

Pork Stuffed with Pear and Ginger

1 lb/454 g pork tenderloin,
   butterflied
3 pears, chopped
1/2 inch/1.25 cm fresh ginger,
   grated
2 green onions, chopped

2 Tbsp/30 ml ricotta or
   cottage cheese
salt and pepper
1/2 cup/125 ml cider or
   apple juice

*Preheat the oven to 400F (200C). "Butterfly" the tenderloin: cut halfway through the width
of the tenderloin for its entire length. Open the butterflied tenderloin and place it between
two sheets of waxed paper. Pound the pork with a rolling pin or empty wine bottle until it
is flattened to 1/4 inch/.6 cm thickness. Mix together the pears, ginger, onions, ricotta, salt
and pepper and spread down the centre of the pork. Roll up and tie the meat with string
at intervals, to keep it together. Place in a baking dish, pour the cider over top, cover and
bake for 20 to 25 minutes. Let stand for 15 minutes. Slice and serve. Serves 4.*

Tuscan Bread Salad

Good chewy bread is essential.

1 loaf good bread, cut into cubes
4 tomatoes, chopped
a sprig of fresh basil, chopped

¹/₂ cup/125 ml olive oil
3 Tbsp/45 ml balsamic vinegar

Toss the bread, tomatoes and basil together. Drizzle the olive oil and vinegar over top and serve. Serves 4 as a side dish.

Locro

This stew is served all over northern Argentina. A day without it is unheard of.

2 Tbsp/30 ml oil
1 lb/454 g pork tenderloin,
   cubed
1 onion, chopped
2 tsp/10 ml turmeric
a pinch of cayenne or
   chili powder
3 cloves garlic, chopped

2 cups/500 ml stock or
   apple juice
2 tsp/10 ml cumin
2 tsp/10 ml dried rosemary
1-28 oz/796 ml tin pumpkin purée
1-14 oz/398 ml tin white beans,
   drained and rinsed
salt and pepper

Heat the oil in a large pot over high heat and add the pork. Cook for 2 to 3 minutes, until browned. Add the onion, turmeric, cayenne and garlic. Reduce the heat to medium and cook for 2 to 3 minutes. Add the remaining ingredients and bring to a boil, stirring constantly. Let everything simmer for 5 more minutes. Season and serve. Serves 4.

Cuban Chicken with Apples and Cilantro

2 Tbsp/30 ml butter
1 tsp/5 ml cumin
1/2 tsp/2.5 ml turmeric
1/2 inch/1.25 cm fresh
  ginger, grated
1 boneless, skinless chicken breast,
  chopped coarse

1 onion, chopped
1 clove garlic, chopped
2 apples, cored and chopped
a handful of cilantro, chopped
salt and pepper

Melt the butter in a large frypan over medium heat. Add the cumin, turmeric, ginger and chicken and cook for 2 minutes, or until the chicken changes colour. Add the onion, garlic and apples and cook for 5 minutes. Stir in the cilantro, season and serve with rice. Serves 2.

Grape Pies

Ridiculously easy, and kids love to do this with you.

12 - 3 inch/7.5 cm frozen tart shells,
  still frozen
1 1/2 cups/375 ml seedless grapes
3 Tbsp/45 ml sugar

1 1/2 Tbsp/22.5 ml flour
2 tsp/10 ml butter
1 egg
1 Tbsp/15 ml water

Preheat the oven to 375F (190C). Fill 6 of the tarts with grapes. Sprinkle each with sugar and flour, and dot with butter. Invert an empty tart shell over each of the filled ones, and press around the edges of the tarts with the tines of a fork to seal the pastry. Beat the egg and water together. Brush the tops of the pies with the egg mixture and bake for 12 to 15 minutes. Makes 6 small pies.

Beef and Daikon Hot Pot

The beef slices best if it's slightly frozen.

2 cups/500 ml club soda
2 tsp/10 ml sugar
3 Tbsp/45 ml vinegar
zest and juice of 1 lemon
3 inches/7.5 cm fresh ginger,
  chopped

1 onion, sliced thin
1 daikon radish, cut into thin strips
1 lb/454 g beef tenderloin,
  sliced very thin
1 head lettuce

Bring the club soda, sugar, vinegar and lemon to a boil in a saucepan over high heat. Pour into a fondue pot or electric frypan and keep it hot. Put the ginger, onion and daikon into the liquid and stir. Dip the beef into the liquid and cook for 10 to 15 seconds. Roll up the beef, some of the daikon, onion and ginger in a lettuce leaf and eat. Fun for 4.

VINEGAR, VALENTINES AND VEGETABLES

ggplants are surely the most beautiful of all vegetables. Plump, shiny, and as overblown as costume jewellery, some are round, some are egg-shaped, some are long and skinny, but no matter how they come they are *so* complete, and *so* perfect, that the most healthy of them might easily be artificial.

Some are large (I've seen giant three-pounders in Greece) and some are small (Thai eggplants grow like berries—no bigger than a hazelnut), but each and every one of them manifests the same innocence and the same absolute inability to deceive. What you see is what you get—the skin says it all. Shiny and firm, as smooth and continuous as a lacquer job on a Porsche—that's a good eggplant. Any blemish on the inside *immediately* shows itself on the outside. They don't wrinkle, and slowly slide into old age and decay. They are not like lemons, which dry and shrink and, as they become ever more juiceless, are regularly reduced in price. They are not like eggs, whose tidy boxes and immaculate shells can suddenly offer the most putrid of surprises. Eggplants are honest and open and thoroughly *decent*, the sort of vegetable that, if one were into marrying vegetables, would make a monumentally boring spouse: beautiful, but demanding.

Cut through an eggplant and you will look in vain for character. No juice, no secret inner structures, no brilliancies of colour, no perfume, and absolutely none of the erotic appeal of, say, a melon, which, opened to the knife immediately invites (almost insists) that your face be buried in it. There is nothing inside an eggplant which speaks of the sun, or the moon, or of hot, or of cold, or of *anything* but slumbering apathy. Unlike the tomato, it has no potential for violence (imagine throwing an eggplant at a politician?), and none of the inherently peaceful virtues of, say, the potato, slices of which, if laid upon eyes sore from weeping (or computer screens), will calm and soothe them.

The eggplant in the kitchen, alone and unadorned, is a backbencher, dull, uninspired and unexciting. But, properly directed, it is outstanding. In the kitchens of the Middle East, of Greece and Italy and Southern France, in the Punjab, Malaysia and China, in Japan and all around the Caspian Sea, eggplants are not only a staple (an ordinary, everyday given of cooking), but they are also revered and loved.

In North America, we are slowly discovering their good qualities. All the biggies in food, people like Wolfgang Puck in Los Angeles, and Celestine Drago and Alice Waters, have made their names with goat cheese, sun-dried tomatoes and—you guessed it—eggplants. In souffles, in *involtini*, in patés and soups, prettied up with colours and in 35 dollar soup plates, eggplants have been the centrefolds of the gourmet magazines for long enough now that they are appearing on the shopping lists of people who shop Friday nights—before they go bowling.

The eggplant's greatest virtue is its ability to *absorb*. Oils, spices, butter, flavours and all the other energies of the kitchen; the eggplant not only takes them, but amplifies and extends them. Eggplants give you feedback —the more you put in, the more you get back. A really good *melitzano* (the eggplant purée popular in Greek restaurants) can contain as many as 18 herbs and spices, all of them slightly improved by association with the bland and sleeping beauty of their host.

In a French restaurant in Vancouver, the

chef makes a magnificent terrine of eggplant: 20 or 30 paper-thin slices interleaved with spices and finely cut roasted peppers, some garlic, a little oil, a little balsamic vinegar and the whole thing baked, cooled and then cut crosswise into dessert-sized slices.

A very cheap dish on the menu of a favourite Chinese restaurant is Spicy Eggplant which gives you a sizeable platter of red brown chunks in a darker brown sauce, sticky, slightly chewy, spicy with fried little killer peppers. If you like it, you will want to order, instead of rice, fried bread—an oval loaf crisp on the outside and soft in the middle—in order to mop up every last drop of the sauce.

A fine Malaysian restaurant serves an outstanding eggplant dish, *Sambal Aubergine*, cooked in a casserole with a thick, spicy gravy based on coconut milk. The chunks of eggplant look like lamb, and even develop the texture of slowly stewed meat, but they are considerably more voluptuous.

At a popular Italian restaurant they simply grill it, douse it with extra virgin olive oil, a lot of pepper, some oregano and a splash of balsamic vinegar. You lay a slice on bread, and bite into it, for immediate understanding of why, in some places, eggplant is called "poor man's steak".

All of these treatments show different aspects of the eggplant—some develop taste, some emphasize texture, some understate and some pretend. The eggplant is basically waiting for you to inspire it, and inspiration is not difficult. Buy one, take it home, admire it, cook it and be delighted. Most cookbooks will give you a procedure for salting it, leaving it for half-an-hour and squeezing it, etcetera, etcetera, etcetera. That was all very necessary 30 years ago when egg-plants had a bitterness, but today's eggplants don't need any of that. They just *need* cooking.

Nobody cooks eggplants more simply than the Sicilians. This is a dish called *Melanzane al Funghetto*, which means eggplant cooked mushroom style, because…well…they also cook mushrooms exactly the same way. It should take you no more than 15 minutes (including cutting the eggplant), and it can be eaten immediately, as a vegetable, or, with a bit more pepper added, as a sauce with spaghetti, or the next day cold, as an antipasto.

Slice one big perfect eggplant as thick as your thumb, then cut it into cubes. Heat four tablespoons (60 ml) of olive oil in a frypan, add the eggplant cubes and cook over high heat, stirring frequently, for five minutes. Turn the heat down to medium, add two cloves of chopped garlic, and cook another five minutes, stirring, or turning over, regularly. Add a good handful of chopped parsley, a teaspoon (five ml) of dried mint (or a couple of stalks of fresh), twice as much pepper as you think advisable, and salt to taste. Stir, cook for another three minutes, sprinkle with lemon juice and there you are.

Next time, fry a halved and sliced onion at the same time as the eggplant for five minutes on high heat. Add the two cloves of chopped garlic and cook for one minute. Add half-a-can of Italian plum tomatoes (or three very ripe fresh ones) and cook for another five minutes. Add the parsley, the mint (or, if you want a change, oregano), the pepper and a table-spoon (15 ml) of vinegar. Cook for five minutes and eat immediately, by itself, or with pasta.

(If you want to be featured in *Chefs Beautiful*, sprinkle the top generously with grated cheese and a few flakes of hot red peppers. Cook in a 350F (177C) oven for 10 minutes.)

Sweet Pepper and Potato Stew

2 Tbsp/30 ml oil
2 anchovy fillets
1 leek, chopped
2 cloves garlic, chopped
12 nugget potatoes, quartered
2 carrots, sliced
1 cup/250 ml corn kernels,
    canned or frozen

2 cups/500 ml stock or water
2 sweet peppers, chopped
a handful of parsley, chopped
1 tsp/5 ml coriander
1 tsp/5 ml cumin
1 tsp/5 ml vinegar

Heat the oil in a large pot and add the anchovies, leek and garlic. Cook for 2 minutes and add the potatoes and carrots. Cook for 2 more minutes. Stir in the corn and stock. Add the peppers, parsley, coriander and cumin and let cook for 10 more minutes. Stir in the vinegar and serve. Serves 2.

Mexican Grilled Turkey

One pot and 15 minutes.

1 1/2 lb/681g raw turkey breast,
    sliced 1/2 inch/1.25 cm thick
salt and pepper
oil
4 Tbsp/60 ml butter

1 red onion, chopped fine
1 cup/250 ml chicken stock
1/4 cup/60 ml white vinegar
2 cups/500 ml mixed greens
    or lettuce

Sprinkle the turkey slices with salt, pepper and a bit of oil. Set aside. Melt the butter in a saucepan over medium heat. Add the onion and cook for 2 to 3 minutes. Add the turkey slices and cook for 5 minutes on each side, until cooked. Remove turkey from the pan (leave the onion in) and add the stock and vinegar. Simmer until reduced or thickened. Arrange the turkey on top of the greens and pour the vinegar sauce over top. Serves 2 as a main course.

Pepper Pitas

8 pita breads
4 Tbsp/60 ml olive oil
a pinch of salt

2 Tbsp/30 ml pepper
2 Tbsp/30 ml parsley

Preheat oven to 400F (200C). Cut the pita into quarters. Brush with oil, and sprinkle with salt, pepper and parsley. Bake until crisp, about 5 minutes. Makes 32 pita wedges.

Cherry Tomatoes and Fresh Basil

Just lovely...

2 Tbsp/30 ml oil
2 cups/500 ml cherry tomatoes,
   whole
3 cloves garlic, chopped

a sprig of basil, chopped
a sprig of thyme, chopped
salt and pepper
1 bay leaf

Heat the oil in a frypan over high heat. Add all of the ingredients, toss and cook for 3 to 4 minutes, until the tomatoes are puffy and just starting to burst. Serves 2.

Salsa Crudo

4 tomatoes, chopped
2 green onions, chopped
a handful of cilantro or
   parsley, chopped
1 Tbsp/15 ml basil or oregano
2 cloves garlic, chopped

1/2 tsp/2.5 ml chili flakes
2 Tbsp/30 ml olive oil
juice of half-a-lemon or lime
1 tsp/5 ml salt
1 tsp/5 ml sugar

Mix all of the ingredients in a bowl and allow to stand for a few minutes. Serve over spaghetti, chicken, fish or with tortilla chips. For a smoother sauce, purée all of the ingredients in a food processor. Makes about 4 cups/1 litre.

Ratatouille

The French classic, in under half-an-hour.

1/4 cup/60 ml olive oil
1 onion, chopped
2 tomatoes, chopped
3 medium-size zucchini,
   chopped
1 medium-size eggplant
   chopped
3 cloves garlic, left whole

1 tsp/5 ml basil
1 tsp/5 ml oregano
1 Tbsp/15 ml tomato paste
1/2 cup/125 ml water
salt and pepper
a handful of parsley,
   chopped

Heat the oil in a saucepan over high heat. Stir in the onion, tomatoes, zucchini and egg-plant. When everything is coated in oil, stir in the garlic, herbs and tomato paste. Add the water, cover and reduce the heat to medium-low. Let simmer for 25 to 30 minutes, or until all of the vegetables have melted down. Season, sprinkle with parsley and serve. Serves 4.

Provençal Baked Vegetables

Just throw it together, bung it in the oven and put up your feet.

1 onion, sliced
1 medium-size eggplant,
   sliced
2 tomatoes, sliced
1 medium-size zucchini,
   sliced
salt and pepper

4 cloves garlic, chopped
1 tsp/5 ml basil
1 tsp/5 ml oregano
1 cup/250 ml mozzarella,
   grated
1/4 cup/60 ml parmesan
3 Tbsp/45 ml oil

Preheat the oven to 350F (177C). Grease an oven-proof dish and place alternate slices of onion, eggplant, tomatoes and zucchini in the dish. Sprinkle with salt, pepper, garlic, basil, oregano, mozzarella and parmesan. Drizzle the oil over top and bake for 25 to 30 minutes, or until the cheese is bubbling and browned and the vegetables have softened. Serves 4.

Basic Vinaigrette

You can add almost anything else—grated cheese, orange juice, garlic, an egg or sherry.

$^1/_2$ cup/125 ml oil
2 Tbsp/30 ml dijon mustard
2 Tbsp/30 ml vinegar or juice
   of half-a-lemon

salt and pepper
a pinch of sugar
1 tsp/5 ml dried herbs, crushed

Put everything in a jar, screw the lid on tight and shake for a couple of seconds,
always shaking well. Makes about $^3/_4$ of a cup/185 ml.

Eggplant Dip with Pepper Pitas

2 medium-size eggplants
2 cloves garlic
1 tsp/5 ml cumin
1 cup/250 ml yoghurt

2 Tbsp/30 ml sesame seeds
3 Tbsp/45 ml cilantro or parsley
juice of 1 lemon
salt and pepper

Bake the eggplants in a 400F (200C) oven for 30 minutes, or until soft. Cut the
eggplants in half and scoop the flesh out. Combine the eggplant flesh and the
remaining ingredients in a food processor and whiz until smooth. Season
and serve with pepper pitas (page 159). Makes about 4 cups/1 litre.

Sautéed Cucumbers

2 Tbsp/30 ml oil
1 cucumber, halved
   and cut into wedges
a bunch of chives, chopped

salt and pepper
$^1/_4$ cup/60 ml cream
a pinch of cayenne
1 Tbsp/15 ml dijon mustard

Heat the oil in a frypan over high heat. Add the cucumbers and chives and cook for
2 to 3 minutes. Season with salt and pepper, then stir in the cream, cayenne
and mustard. Toss and serve. Serves 2.

WINE, WOMEN AND WRONG

Whatever I've learned in the kitchen has come from one—and occasionally all—of these three influences: wine, women and wrong.

Wine has eased my inhibitions; women have given me charity, kindness, kisses and encouragement; and when things went wrong, one or both of them were there to comfort me, and convince me that mistakes were not only human, but essential to any serious learning.

If you mistake the salt for the sugar, it's hard to do much more than throw it out. If you burn the garlic, you *have* to throw it out. Baking and the making of pastry are arts almost *pharmaceutically* precise, to be learned with care and tedium and the end products are either magnificent or drearily ordinary. But, in most other dishes (perhaps efforts is a better name than dishes) the odd mistake doesn't matter.

Whatever happens is a variation on a theme. The home economists with their precisely levelled teaspoons, and the measurers with their scales and their thermometers—they're not enjoying their cooking; they're painting by numbers, and waiting for judgement. Even worse, they judge themselves. They look at the beautiful pictures in the middle of the cookbook and know that what they've made just isn't good enough. It doesn't look like the picture *and* it doesn't glisten and shine *and* it has burnt bits at the edges and stuff stuck to the pan. So they take it to the table and apologize profusely. They're sad about it, there's no joy and they're back in Grade One

and Miss Wilson is judging them ("Trees are *green*, not purple…").

So make mistakes and learn to improvise. If you haven't got thyme, use rosemary, or oregano. No butter? Use oil. Don't like pork? Use turkey breast. No vinegar? Use lemon juice. Can't find the breadcrumbs? Try crushed corn flakes. Out of white wine? Use apple juice. Veal stock? N*obody* has veal stock, so use chicken stock.

The only things you can't cheat on, or fake are the really important ones, like cream. There is no such thing as low-fat cream and the whole purpose of cream in cooking is to give things a smooth, luxurious texture which will carry the flavours softly to your palate. So use real cream. And, no matter what they do to margarine, it will never have the same flavour or texture as butter, and most margarines will clog up your arteries with the residues of hydrogenated fats.

Be generous with seasonings (except salt, which you can always add later), remember that Julia Child is remembered most for dropping the chicken, not cooking it, and never, ever forget that: One; Martha Stewart is a corporation, and two; it's *your* kitchen, and it should be *fun*.

And finally, I learned a lot of my cooking from my grandmother, who never read a book in her life. She was illiterate, but could she cook!

Cranberry and Pork

If you haven't got pork, then use chicken or turkey.

$^3/_4$ lb/340 g pork tenderloin,
   cubed
2 Tbsp/30 ml flour
2 Tbsp/30 ml oil
1 onion, chopped

1 cup/250 ml white wine
$^3/_4$ cup/185 ml cranberries
3 Tbsp/45 ml honey
a sprig of fresh basil, chopped

Coat the pork in flour. Heat the oil in a saucepan over high heat. Add the pork and cook for 2 minutes, until browned. Add the onion and cook a further 2 minutes, or until the onion has softened. Add the white wine, cranberries, honey and basil and stir. Turn the heat down to a simmer, cover and let cook 20 minutes. Serve over rice. Serves 2.

Chicken with Sultanas

A traditional Hungarian wedding dish.

2 Tbsp/30 ml oil
2 boneless, skinless chicken breasts
$^1/_2$ cup/125 ml sultanas or raisins
1 lemon, thinly sliced

$^1/_2$ cup/125 ml apple juice
1 Tbsp/15 ml vinegar
$^1/_4$ cup/60 ml red wine

Heat the oil in a frypan over high heat. Add the chicken breasts and raisins. Cook for 2 to 3 minutes on each side, until browned, then add the lemon and apple juice, cover and let cook for 5 minutes. Reduce the heat to medium and remove the chicken from the pan. Add the remaining ingredients and cook until the sauce is slightly thickened. Pour the sauce over the chicken and serve. Serves 2.

Italian Apples with Almonds and White Wine

Mmmmmmmmm...

2 Tbsp/30 ml butter

4 apples, peeled,
   cored and cut into slices

zest and juice of 1 lemon

2 cloves

1/2 cup/125 ml brandy
   or whiskey

1/4 cup/60 ml sugar

1/2 cup/125 ml sweet white wine

a pinch of cinnamon

whipped cream

3/4 cup/185 ml sliced almonds,
   toasted

Melt the butter in a large frypan over medium heat. Add the apples, lemon and cloves and cook for 2 minutes. Add the whiskey, sugar, white wine and cinnamon and cook until a thin syrup forms. Remove from heat, top with whipped cream and almonds and serve. Serves 4.

Prawns with Feta

Straight from a little bar in Piraeus—the essence of Greece.

2 Tbsp/30 ml oil

1 onion, chopped

2 cloves garlic, chopped

4 tomatoes, chopped

1/2 cup/125 ml white wine

2 lbs/1 kg raw prawns, peeled

3/4 cup/185 ml feta cheese

pepper

a handful of parsley, chopped

a sprig of fresh mint, chopped

Heat the oil in a frypan over high heat. Add the onion and garlic and cook for 2 minutes. Stir in the tomatoes and wine and bring to a boil. Reduce the heat and stir in the prawns. Cook for 2 to 3 minutes, crumble the feta over top, add the pepper and let everything cook until the feta is melted and the prawns have just turned pink. Serve on rice, sprinkled with parsley and mint. Serves 4.

Good Queen Bess Mulled Wine

3 cups/750 ml red wine

1 cup/250 ml port

$^1/_2$ cup/125 ml cognac

zest of 1 lemon

a pinch of cinnamon

a pinch of nutmeg

6 cloves

Combine all of the ingredients in a saucepan and heat until steaming over medium heat. Do not boil. Serve immediately. Makes about 4 cups/1 litre and serves 6.

X-STASY

Restaurants in Japan frequently have display cases outside filled with plastic replicas of the dishes they serve inside. The replicas are beautiful, faithfully reproducing in every detail the originals. But, you can't *eat* them.

And, (to some people), Madonna, Arnold Schwarzenegger and Demi Moore look very nice on the outside. But, just as in the case of the plastic food replicas, looks aren't everything. Food, more than any other of the sensory pleasures, demands *all* of our senses to make it perfect. Particularly, when it comes to eating strawberries.

One billion pounds of California strawberries arrive in British Columbia every year, during every month (except January and February). And, they're fine, they're the best you can eat, *unless* it happens to be late June and early July. Then, the fields are full of local strawberries, and *these* strawberries are full of juice; too juicy and too ripe and too delicate to move (very carefully) any further than a few miles. Strawberries just on the edge of being too ripe, with the same rich colour and the same juicy texture all the way through. These are indeed *strawberries*: the sort of unforgettable experience which sets the standard for every other strawberry you will ever eat, and makes you content to wait out the eleven months they are not in season.

I sit in the sun and eat a pound of local strawberries almost every day they are available. I also eat new local potatoes every day, cooked with wild mint that grows on a vacant lot down the street. I eat local wild salmon for the two months it's in season, fresh halibut, local silver smelts and *anything* else I can find that is in season and doesn't have to be driven hundreds of miles in a refrigerated truck. Eating local is what travellers do in France, and Thailand, and anywhere else that's worth visiting, but it seems to be a hard habit to cultivate right here at home.

But let's get back to strawberries, local fresh strawberries. Did you know that ninety percent of strawberries are eaten raw, and that the most popular use of the other ten percent is in strawberry shortcake? There *are* interesting alternatives.

Like a salad of sliced strawberries and thinly sliced cucumber is as spectacular as any store bought cake—the cucumber laid out in a ring around the edge of a plate, then half-covered with a smaller ring of sliced strawberries, then a smaller ring of cucumber and more strawberries right up to the centre, where a whole fat strawberry sits proud, and the whole thing drizzled with a simple vinaigrette of oil, lemon juice and coarsely ground pepper. Fresh spinach, washed and well-dried, with quartered strawberries and a dressing of yoghurt, pepper and chopped green dill; four fat strawberries arranged on a lettuce leaf and dressed with a honey, mint and balsamic vinegar vinaigrette. (You do have to remember that a fresh, really ripe fruit has a lot of available sweetness, and that sweetness is emphasized by the addition of something mildly acidic, like lemon juice, or spicy, like fresh ground pepper.)

Strawberries also go very well with white meat and fish. Cook a boneless chicken breast (with the skin removed), with a small piece of butter, and two or three small, whole dried hot red peppers in a frypan over medium heat. A minute before it's done, add the green parts (thinly sliced) of a bunch of spring onions, two (or four) pinches of pepper and a few drops of vinegar. Cook for a minute, then take out the chicken and stir in two tablespoons (30 ml) of yoghurt and a dozen or so strawberries. The sauce goes on top of the chicken or underneath—that's your choice.

Halibut, with its dense, mild, but firm, flesh is the nicest of fishes with strawberries. Steam it in a frypan with a tight fitting lid— no more than a quarter-inch (.5 cm) of water, a tablespoon (15 ml) of butter and the fish lightly salted and peppered. Cook eight minutes for each inch of thickness, then take off the lid, cover the fish with sliced strawberries, cook another minute with the lid on, then take out the fish, add half-a-glass of white wine to the pan, with a bit of chopped parsley and another lump of butter. Boil it until it looks a little sticky, add some more sliced strawberries, mash them down a little for no more than thirty seconds, pour out on to a plate and put the fish on top.

It sounds almost *sacrilegious* to think of fresh strawberries in a barbecue sauce, but there's always a few in the bottom of the box that are not the finest. Hull them and mash them in a pan with equal quantities of vinegar, soy sauce and sugar, with two cloves of garlic, finely chopped, and a healthy sprinkle of hot red pepper. Slowly bring to a boil, stirring constantly, then stir in one tablespoon (15 ml) of cornstarch, mixed in smoothly with two tablespoons (30 ml) of whatever alcohol you have in the cupboard. Remove from the heat as soon as it looks slightly sticky and translucent.

A wide-mouthed jar with a lid, four pounds (two kg) of very ripe strawberries and a litre (four cups) of vinegar (plain white vinegar is perfectly adequate, but wine vinegar is better) will make you Christmas presents that will bring back summer in the middle of winter. Put the strawberries in the jar, mash them down with a wooden spoon, and stir in the vinegar. Let the jar stand at room temperature (but not in direct sunlight) for a week. Strain off the vinegar which by now has a magnificent colour, boil it for five minutes and strain again (through a piece of cloth). Pour into small, sterilized bottles (fifteen minutes in the oven at 300°F (150C) is the easiest way) and cork or screw the caps on. Make some labels *delicately* pointing out that this is homemade, and is based on centuries of inherited knowledge. Store until an appropriate time comes along for gift giving.

And, finally, for the eighty percent who *don't* want to cook strawberries, a few alternatives to cream. Dip them in red wine and then, just the tips in sugar, or sprinkle them with Cointreau and a few drops of orange juice.

Raspberry and Mint Fool

They sit and drool over raspberry fool.

2 cups/500 ml raspberries
a handful of mint leaves
a splash of rum

1/2 cup/125 ml whipped cream
icing sugar

In a food processor, whiz together the raspberries, mint and rum until smooth. Fold in the whipped cream with a fork and sweeten to taste with the icing sugar. Serves 2.

Pears with Gorgonzola

Straight from God's personal cookbook.

2 pears, cored and thinly sliced
1/4 lb/113 g gorgonzola or
  blue cheese, crumbled
zest and juice of 1 lemon

1/2 cup/125 ml almonds,
  chopped
a sprig of basil, chopped

Preheat oven to 400F (200C). Lay the pear slices on a baking sheet and place a lump of cheese on each. Sprinkle with lemon, almonds and basil. Bake for 10 minutes, or until cheese is melted and nuts are browned. Serves 2.

Strawberries and Pepper

Just try it once.

1 pint strawberries
sour cream or yoghurt

pepper

Dip the strawberries into the sour cream or yoghurt, grind fresh pepper over top and enjoy! Serves 2.

Summer Pudding

No cooking, no stove, just plain lovely.

$^1/_2$ lb/227 g raspberries
  or strawberries
$^1/_2$ lb/227 g blueberries
$^1/_2$ tsp/2.5 ml butter,
  for greasing the bowl

3 Tbsp/45 ml sugar
$^1/_2$ loaf sliced bread,
  crusts removed
whipped cream

Mix the berries and sugar together. Line a buttered bowl with the slices of bread, making sure every bit is covered and there are no holes. Fill with the fruit and place more bread slices on top. Cover with a plate which fits inside the bowl and place a weight on top. Allow to sit overnight in the fridge. Turn out onto a plate and serve with whipped cream. Serves 4.

Bruschetta with Fruit

1 cup/250 ml ricotta or
  cottage cheese
2 Tbsp/30 ml orange juice
1 baguette, sliced finger-thick
2 peaches, sliced or 1 tin
  peaches, drained

6 strawberries, sliced
12 grapes, halved
4 Tbsp/60 ml brown sugar
a sprig of fresh mint

Mix the ricotta and orange juice together. Toast the bread and spread the cheese on the warm bread, topping with slices of fruit and sprinkled with sugar. Serve garnished with mint leaves. Serves 4.

YEARNINGS

"You have to make it with love…" says Tita, the sad-eyed, tearful and unfulfilled heroine of Alfonso Arau's beautiful film, *Like Water For Chocolate*. She is a born cook, a loving and caressing cook, a beauty, but unfortunately the last born daughter of a Mexican family whose tradition forbids her to marry. She must stay home and look after Mama, until Mama should die. Tita is the kind of romantic who loves once—for life. Her love is Pedro, and Mama, a right purse-mouthed, proper and sadistically virtuous bitch, forces Pedro to marry Tita's sister, and then makes Tita bake the cake for the occasion.

She weeps into the mixing bowl, and her tears are so strong, so charged with emotion, that the wedding guests are all sick. And, so it goes from then on, the whole film a melodrama of food and feudin', fightin', fartin', and makin' love. Babies are born on kitchen tables; there is a spectacular union between another sister and a mustachioed revolutionary on the back of a galloping horse; there is love by lantern light and by moonlight, on river banks, in outhouses and in whorehouses. There are passions of such intensity that they set light to beds, to houses, and to people's lives.

Like Water For Chocolate is a romantic fable, almost an opera, which despite its cautions ("nudity, some violence, suggestive scenes…") is a gentle, loving and significant film. Quietly tucked in amongst the illogicalities of hormonally inspired behaviour are political messages, grandmotherly advice and of course, recipes—not just kitchen recipes, but good old-fashioned kitchen table wisdom.

Arau makes food an allegory for love—"without passion, it's nothing", but it's not exactly a *food* movie. There are no lingering closeups of artificial, stylized centrefold dishes, and none of the *in* jokes so dear to the food mafia. The film's title comes from the Mexican recipe for hot chocolate—the water must be at a rolling boil to do justice to the grated chocolate, and anybody in a state of aroused readiness is considered to be "like water for chocolate". Apart from that, all food in the film is treated as an essential to life and a doorway to all sensory pleasures.

The cookbook which starts the film and the only thing left in the ruins of a burned house, is a cultural testament, a form of immortality which we all recognize, in such simple ways as treasuring a family recipe for spaghetti sauce, or recalling, even incorrectly, the fabulous dinner we had at cousin Samantha's wedding.

When the lovers finally unite (and ignite), that too is a simple and unavoidable statement of the nature of food as the ultimate performance art—something which can never be repeated in exactly the same form, and something of a dignity which is seldom fully recognized outside the boundaries of intellectual analysis. They waited *years* to do it, through other marriages and other loves, and when they finally did, it was a transcendental experience, unique and perfect unto itself, in its own time. And, that's no more, and no less, than a well made dinner should be.

We bring flowers to our lovers as a manifestation of love, and most often we put them in water, in vases and we admire them. Tita, forbidden the roses which her lover brings, is told to destroy them. She does destroy them, but in her own way. She cooks them, actually transmutes them into a dish with quails, and as she stirs, and dreams, and cries, the essence of her passion is incorporated into the sauce. At the table, as the company eats, they absorb this passion, and suddenly, *en masse*, are overcome by their own unfulfilled passions and desires, and rush—in couples—to the nearest horizontal surface.

The politically correct will find many faults in the simplicity of this basic equation: food equals love equals passion equals immortality. But, there is hardly one of us who is not familiar with the basic "You are what you eat", and who cannot quote it to reinforce a specific position, all the way from the cholesterol crusaders to the spiritual dieters. *Like Water For Chocolate* sends its audiences back to the real world with a special awareness of the catholicism of joy available in food, as a social stimulant, a total sensory pleasure and a basic creative process.

This may sound like a rationale for my particular way of earning a living, and indeed it is—I came out of the theatre with my faith in food as a transcendental experience (like all true believers I have occasional doubts) fully restored. But today's food—like today's sex—analyzed, counted and constantly evaluated, has lost much of its original pleasure, and is in serious danger of reverting to the fundamentalist concept of original sin.

Like Water For Chocolate is a film that does a great deal to recreate true family values—not the nasty puritanical joyless family values of the Ronald Reagan era—but a re-recognition of the pleasures, the *necessity*, of sitting down together at the table and enjoying it.

Persian Stew

1 1/2 lb/681 g lamb or beef,
    cut into bite-size pieces
2 Tbsp/30 ml flour
2 Tbsp/30 ml butter
2 Tbsp/30 ml oil
1 onion, chopped
1 clove garlic, chopped
1/2 tsp/2.5 ml cinnamon

2 cups/500 ml mushrooms,
1 tsp/5 ml salt
1/2 tsp/2.5 ml pepper
1/4 cup/60 ml sherry or
    apple juice
1 cup/250 ml water
juice of half-a-lemon, quartered
2 egg yolks, beaten smooth

Dust the meat pieces in flour. Heat the butter and oil in a saucepan over medium heat. Add the meat and cook for 2 minutes, until browned. Add the onion and cook for 3 to 4 minutes. Stir in the remaining ingredients, except for the egg yolks, and cover. Simmer 25 minutes, quickly stir in the egg yolks and serve immediately over rice. Serves 4.

Bannock

Great fun for kids.

1 cup/250 ml flour
1/2 tsp/2.5 ml salt
1 1/2 tsp/7.5 ml baking powder

1 tsp/5 ml sugar
1 tsp/5 ml butter or oil
1 cup/250 ml milk

Mix the flour, salt, baking powder and sugar together in a bowl. Add the oil and milk, stirring until you have a stiff batter. Dust your hands with flour and press the batter into a flat cake about 1/2 an inch/1.25 cm thick. Poke a hole in the middle (so it looks like a big donut). Heat a lightly greased frypan over high heat for 1 minute, then turn it to low. Place the bannock in the pan, cover and cook for 5 minutes. Flip, cook for 5 more minutes, and then cook a further 10 minutes on each side (cook about 35 minutes altogether). Eat immediately with lots of butter and jam or peanut butter. Serves 2.

New Potatoes with Mint

1/4 cup/60 ml butter
1 tsp/5 ml salt
1/2 tsp/2.5 ml pepper

2 Tbsp/30 ml fresh mint, chopped
2 cups/500 ml new potatoes or nugget potatoes, cooked

Melt the butter in a small saucepan over medium heat. Season with salt and pepper and stir in the chopped mint. Add the cooked potatoes, coat them well and cook, covered, over low heat for 5 minutes. Serves 2.

Poor Man's Hot and Sour Soup

If you like things really sour, just add more vinegar.

4 cups/1 litre water or stock
1 skinless, boneless chicken breast, chopped
1 clove garlic, chopped
3 chilis
1/2 a red pepper, chopped
1/2 pkg medium tofu, cut into bite-size pieces

2 Tbsp/30 ml soy sauce
1 inch/2.5 cm fresh ginger, grated
1 onion, chopped
4 mushrooms, sliced
2 Tbsp/30 ml cornstarch
6 Tbsp/90 ml vinegar
2 green onions, chopped fine

Bring the water or stock to a boil and add the chicken, garlic, chilis, red pepper and tofu. Bring to a boil again and add the soy sauce, ginger, onion and mushrooms. Let everything simmer for 5 minutes. Mix the cornstarch with the vinegar and pour into the soup. Bring the soup to a boil again and serve sprinkled with green onions. Serves 4.

Pain Perdu

A New Orleans version of french toast.

3 Tbsp/45 ml oil

3 eggs

2 Tbsp/30 ml rum or whiskey

1 Tbsp/15 ml milk

3 Tbsp/45 ml sugar

zest of half-a-lemon

6 slices bread, stale

icing sugar

Heat the oil in a frypan over medium heat. In a bowl, beat together the eggs, rum, milk, sugar and lemon zest. Dredge the bread slices in this mixture and place carefully into the hot frypan. Fry 3 to 4 minutes each side, or until golden brown. Sprinkle with icing sugar, and serve with butter and maple syrup. Serves 2.

Sugar Pastry with Rum Bananas

Saturday afternoon, and it's raining. The kids will love you if you let them do it. The magic words are: "These are wonderful..."

2 cups/500 ml ready-made
bread dough

2 Tbsp/30 ml butter

2 Tbsp/30 ml sugar

1/2 tsp/2.5 ml cinnamon

3 bananas, mashed

juice of 1 orange

3 Tbsp/45 ml rum

1 Tbsp/15 ml brown sugar

icing sugar

Preheat the oven to 375F (190C). Roll out the bread dough as thin as possible and spread with butter, sugar and cinnamon. Spread mashed banana on top and sprinkle with orange juice and rum. Roll up the dough into a loaf shape and sprinkle it with brown sugar. Place in a greased loaf tin or baking dish. Bake for 10 to 15 minutes or until it has risen and has turned light brown. Dust with icing sugar, slice and serve. Serves 4.

Baked Apples

4, 6, even 8, they take no longer to cook.

2 large apples, cored, not peeled
a handful of raisins
1 Tbsp/15 ml fresh ginger, grated

juice of half-a-lemon
3 Tbsp/45 ml brown sugar
1 Tbsp/15 ml butter

Heat the oven to 350F (177C). Place the apples in a greased baking dish and stuff them with the raisins. Sprinkle the ginger, lemon juice and brown sugar over top and dot with butter. Bake for 25 to 30 minutes, until soft. Serves 2.

Fruit Clafoutis

A french sort of upside-down cake, cooked in a pot, which uses any fruit in season.

3 eggs
2 Tbsp/30 ml sugar
1 cup/250 ml flour

1 cup/250 ml milk
2-14 oz/398 ml tins cherries
(or any other fruit), drained

Preheat the oven to 350F (177C). Beat the eggs in a large bowl with the sugar, flour and milk to make a smooth batter. Put the cherries into a greased baking dish and pour the batter over top of the fruit. Bake for 30 minutes, or until the batter is puffed up and baked through. Serve sprinkled with a little more sugar, or with a dollop of whipped cream. Serves 4.

ZUCCHINI, ZARZUELA AND ZENOBIA JONES

Zenobia Jones travelled on trains, and because she was small, *and* drop dead gorgeous, men talked to her. She wore glasses with important and serious looking frames, so they almost always talked to her about intellectual matters, or, to be precise, matters they *thought* were intellectual. But, what they all really wanted to do was buy her breakfast, or lunch, in the dining car. She, being polite, young and hungry, usually accepted with a smile. Most of them discovered halfway through breakfast, or lunch, that they were seriously out of their intellectual depth, she being exceptionally smart and well-informed. But they plodded on, lust—particularly male lust—having very little sensitivity, and managed (most of them, anyway) to ask for a phone number. Which she gave them (of course, it was an invented phone number just like her invented name).

Zenobia Jones she most certainly wasn't. *Very* occasionally (but not while I lived with her) she gave her real name and phone number, and they would visit her, hoping, at the least (having seen her appetite) for a good dinner and at the most, a breakfast. But, they were usually disappointed. She lived on a steady diet of Big Macs; every Sunday she bought seven, ate one, froze the others and nuked one every evening, unless she had a dinner guest, when she nuked two, and opened another beer.

She spent her money on books, and her planning involved seeing just how many of them she could stuff into her apartment. Every wall was used for books, and every cupboard in the kitchen. She ate the same way they put gas in her car; no muss, no fuss, and almost no dishes.

It worked for her, but not for me. My basic definition of a home is *never* having to send out for anything, and being able to whip up a meal in half-an-hour, drunk, sober, midday or midnight, and no matter how many unexpected visitors arrive. Which is not really very difficult, when you have a carefully thought out store cupboard. It doesn't have to be big, and it doesn't have to be expensive.

The things I consider essential (call it an urban desert island survival kit) are: a big brown onion, a can of sockeye salmon, a can of beans, a can of Italian tomatoes, a piece of cheddar cheese, a large green cabbage, a large carrot, a head of garlic, half-a-dozen bread rolls kept frozen in a ziplock bag, a jar of good chunky peanut butter, a dozen eggs, some hot sauce and a couple of big juicy oranges. Also, any kind of pasta, a box of the best soup or stock cubes you can find, and a piece of root ginger. T*hat's it*.

You should have butter or oil or whatever you use for cooking fat, pepper and salt and just one herb like thyme or oregano or rosemary. A bottle of wine will make almost any meal an occasion, but beer will do in a pinch. For a $50 investment (which won't quite buy four pizzas) you have a survival kit which will a: last out the biggest snowstorm, b: dazzle whoever happens to be holed up with you and, c: turn you, almost effortlessly, into the sort of legendary cook of whom people say "just walked in the door, opened the fridge and there was dinner".

The recipes? T*he essence of successful survival is improvisation*. The pasta goes into a pot of boiling water and you have 12 minutes before it's cooked. Chop an onion, fry it a bit over medium heat, add some chopped garlic, mash in half the can of tomatoes and a teaspoon (five ml) of the one herb you have and by the time the pasta's drained you have a quick, fresh, instant Italian-style tomato sauce.

Fed up with Italian? Then don't add the tomatoes to the onion and garlic. Instead, stir in two tablespoons (30 ml) of peanut butter and a few shakes of hot sauce. Thin it out a bit with beer, wine or water, mix it in with the cooked, hot noodles, and suddenly it's almost Tan Tan noodles, a Northern Chinese dish, spicy, hot and filling.

Almost is a key word in improvisation cooking. You don't need a tall white hat and things don't have to be perfect. While Marcella Hazan is to be admired, cooking is an intensely personal art form, an adult version of finger painting, and the best recipes are as vague as country directions ("down the road a piece you turn left, right?").

So, take the tomatoes, the onions and the garlic we cooked for the Italian pasta sauce, add some hot sauce, thin it out in the pan with a little orange juice (or wine, or beer) and crack two eggs into the middle of it. Put the lid on, and cook over medium heat until the eggs are cooked. Almost Huevos Rancheros.

Don't like poached eggs? Then crack the eggs into a cup, beat them with a fork, and stir them into the tomato/onion garlic mix. Almost *piperade*, a French dish.

None of these appeal to you? Then dissolve a couple of soup cubes in two cups (500 ml) of hot water, add them to the tomato and garlic mix, and bring to the boil. Squeeze in a little orange juice, a few good shakes of pepper, some grated carrot and a few cabbage leaves sliced very thinly. Cook it for two minutes over high heat, then gently stir in the salmon. What is it? Fish soup, not *bouillabaisse*, not *halashle* or chowder; it's just fish soup and if you want to add a little grated ginger, it's still fish soup but almost Chinese, and if you add some cooked noodles and a bit more hot sauce and a spoonful of peanut butter it's very close to being a Korean fish soup.

Still lusting for pizza? Slice the bread rolls crosswise into finger-thick slices. Toast them very lightly in the toaster oven, put a good spoonful of the tomato and onion mix on top, lay a thin slice of cheese on top, sprinkle with hot sauce and toast some more until the cheese melts. It's not pizza, and it's not *bruschetta*, but it's quick and it's good.

Peanut butter instead of the cheese? Fine. Canned salmon instead of the peanut butter? Fine. Peanut butter *and* salmon? Very nice, particularly if you lay a very thin slice of onion on top of everything to brown in the toaster oven.

None of this is *haute cuisine*. At best it's "mess about" cooking, but it's cheap, it's easy, and *shared* with somebody else, is much more rewarding than take-out.

And much better than a Big Mac.

Zucchini and Mint Salad

Fresh and bright, even better with butter.

2 Tbsp/30 ml oil
1 large zucchini, cut into coins,
   or half a dozen very small ones
1 tsp/5 ml salt

$1/2$ tsp/2.5 ml pepper
a handful of fresh mint, chopped
zest and juice of 1 lemon

Heat the oil in a frypan over medium heat. Add the zucchini, sprinkle with salt and pepper and cook for 4 to 5 minutes, stirring, until tender. Add the remaining ingredients, season and serve warm or cold. Serves 4 as a side dish.

Zucchini with Apples and Dill

2 Tbsp/30 ml butter
1 onion, chopped
2 large zucchini, cubed
1 apple, cored and chopped

$1/4$ cup/60 ml dill, chopped
juice of half-a-lemon
salt and pepper

Melt the butter in a frypan over medium heat. Add the onion and zucchini and cook for 3 minutes. Add the apple, dill and lemon juice and cook for a further 3 minutes. Season and serve. Serves 4.

Dolce Mio

juice of 1 orange
1 cup/250 ml sultanas or
   golden raisins

a splash of marsala or port
vanilla ice cream

Place the juice, raisins and marsala in a saucepan and simmer for 10 minutes or so, or until the raisins have plumped up nicely. Pour over the ice cream and serve. Serves 4.

Vegetarian Daube

Olives become very bitter when cooked, so just stir them in at the last minute.

2 Tbsp/30 ml oil
1 zucchini, cubed
1 onion, chopped
3 cloves garlic, chopped
2 carrots, chopped
2 tomatoes, chopped

a sprig of fresh thyme or
   rosemary or 1 tsp/5 ml dried
zest of 1 orange
2 anchovy fillets
1 1/2 cups/375 ml red wine
12 black olives

Heat the oil in a large pot over high heat. Add the zucchini, onion and garlic and cook for 2 to 3 minutes. Add the remaining ingredients except the olives, bring to a boil and reduce the heat to medium. Cover and cook for 15 minutes. Stir in the olives and serve. Serves 4.

Zarzuela

A Spanish Bouillabaise.

2 Tbsp/30 ml oil
1 onion, chopped
5 cloves garlic, chopped
3 tomatoes, chopped
2 bay leaves
2 cups/500 ml fish or chicken stock,
   or 1 cup/250 ml water and
   1 cup/250 ml clam juice
a handful of parsley, chopped

1 fillet white fish, cubed
a pinch of saffron, soaked in
   1/2 cup/125 ml hot water
12 mussels
12 clams
1/4 cup/60 ml sherry
1/4 cup/60 ml Pernod or
   brandy, even rye whiskey

Heat the oil in a large pot over high heat. Add the onion, garlic, tomatoes and bay leaves and cook for 5 minutes. Add the stock and parsley and bring to a boil. Add the fish, cook for 3 minutes, then add the saffron (with the water it soaked in), shellfish, sherry and Pernod. Simmer for 4 to 5 minutes, or until the shellfish have opened, and serve. Serves 2.

Ziti with Sausage and Tomatoes

Ziti is a pasta, kind of like macaroni, only longer, thinner and completely straight and it cooks very quickly.

2 Italian sausages, sliced into coins
1 onion, chopped
1 green pepper, chopped
2 tomatoes, chopped
a sprig of fresh basil, chopped

4 cups/1 litre cooked ziti, or
    any other pasta, drained
parmesan
salt and pepper

Put the sausages in a frypan over high heat. Cook for 3 minutes, stirring, so both sides get browned. Add the onion, green pepper and tomatoes and cook for 5 minutes, until the tomatoes start to turn mushy. Remove from heat and toss with the basil, ziti and parmesan. Season and serve. Serves 2.

Orange and Lemon Chicken

Valentine's Day, any day.

2 boneless, skinless
    chicken breasts
2 Tbsp/30 ml flour
2 Tbsp/30 ml oil
$1/2$ an onion, chopped
2 sticks celery, chopped
2 slices fresh ginger, chopped

zest and juice of 1 orange
zest and juice of 1 lemon
a sprig of fresh mint, chopped
1 cup/250 ml white wine or
    apple juice
salt and pepper

Coat the chicken breasts in flour. Heat the oil in a frypan over high heat. Add the chicken and cook 2 minutes on each side, until nicely browned. Add the onion, celery and ginger and cook a further 4 minutes, until softened. Stir in the orange and lemon juices and zest, mint and wine. Season, reduce the heat to low, cover and simmer for 5 minutes. Serve with extra mint. Serves 2.